MOTIVATING PEOPLE

Kurt Hanks

Crisp Publications

Motivating People

Kurt Hanks

CREDITS
Contributors: **Jerry Pulsipher, Lisa Vermillion**
Editor: **Lisa Vermillion**
Illustrations: **Kurt Hanks**

Copyright © 1991 by Crisp Publications, Inc.
Printed in the United States of America

Distribution to the U.S. Trade:

National Book Network, Inc.
4720 Boston Way
Lanham, MD 20706
1-800-462-6420

Library of Congress Catalog Card Number 90-84074
Hanks, Kurt
Motivating People
ISBN 1-56052-085-X

This book is printed on recyclable paper with soy ink.

PRINTED WITH SOY INK

MOTIVATING PEOPLE

Contents

Read This First

Motivation is everybody's problem. It doesn't matter what we do in life, or where we think we fall in the pecking order, we still have the need, a critical need, to motivate others.

Consider a few situations where you might find yourself in need of some good motivational techniques.

• Your employee just won't meet the required production deadlines.

• Your younger children continually shirk their chores, or your teenager won't do the assigned homework.

• As the leader of a group, you need to get things rolling for a fund raiser.

• Your superiors are always on your tail— and you need to motivate them to get off.

• You are a salesman and you want to motivate your clients to buy.

• You are a teacher and would like to motivate your students to do better.

Sometimes it does help to read the instructions.

And that's only the beginning. From the time when we get up in the morning to when we go to bed at night, we run into dozens of situations where we need to motivate others. If you are frustrated in your efforts (and who isn't?), this book can make the difference. It contains scores of ideas on how to effectively motivate others. You don't have to use all the ideas. Pick and choose those which best fit your circumstance. One or two ideas, well applied, can revolutionize how others react to you.

For many people, getting others to do things is like pulling teeth. It's the low point of the day for the motivator and the "motivatee." But with good motivational techniques, like those described in this book, other people will not only do what we ask, but they will thank us for the privilege!

It's hard to talk about a subject unless everyone agrees on the meanings of key words. To help avoid such problems, I'm giving some working definitions of a few words you'll find over and over in the book:

• **Manager** A person who manages the work, or a portion of the lives, of other people. Examples: business managers, group leaders, teachers, salespeople, parents. A Manager is any person who has a need to motivate others—or in other words, any one of us!

• **Motivation** The process of getting other people to do what you want them to do.

• **Motivator** Any person who tries to apply the Motivation process, whether successfully or not. All Motivators are also Managers.

• **Organization** A group of any size or makeup. Examples: companies, both large and small; shops, sections, and departments within companies; government agencies; service groups; church groups; youth groups; schools and classrooms; families.

• **Production/Productivity** The process whereby things get done. Production can apply to problems as diverse as getting cars manufactured in the factory to getting beds made in the home. The person who stimulates Production is the Manager or Motivator; the person who carries out the Production is the Worker.

• **Worker/Employee/Motivatee** Any person who has a need to be motivated. Any person who is in a subordinate position to a Manager. Examples: company employees, service group volunteers, students, children in the home.

A reader may feel uncomfortable with my global use of the pronoun *He* throughout the book. When he/she encounters *He* when s/he thinks it should be *She* or *He/She*, she or he may remember how painful it was to read this paragraph and accept sincere apologies from this author for the frequent use of the pronoun *He*, when he really meant *He or She*.

The People Problem

The whole earth is crawling with them. They get into our food. They meddle with our work. They influence our travel. They make us miserable. Sometimes they make us happy. What are they? They are us! People!

We can't live with them—but we can't live without them either. Ninety percent of our needs are met in some part by others: for example, food, self-esteem, security, sex.

People

People take up the greatest portion of our operating budget. They make our decisions—and carry them through. They create most of our problems. And solve them.

The people problem is even more complicated than it looks at first glance. Put two trees together, side by side, and all you have is two trees standing beside each other. But put two people together and you have an interaction. Every person in this universe is totally unique. And every combination of people creates a whole new formula.

People are the source of most of our problems. But they also give us our solutions.

Too bad we can't all head for the hills and be hermits. But that doesn't work either, because we're hopelessly interdependent.

People Need Other People

We need each other in order to live—in order to be comfortable.

13

That's as true in an organization as it is in life. Everything critical to functioning in any organization is dependent on the actions of others. Whether you are a business manager, a salesperson, a teacher, or a parent, you need this interaction in order to succeed.

Every manager is dependent on his workers—if he couldn't influence them, he'd be up a creek. He'd have to rely on others, but without influence he'd have no way of assuring that his own needs would be met.

Motivation Is the Answer

Without motivation there is no change. No learning. No action. And, most important of all, without motivation there are no results.

Fortunately, we can have influence. Motivation is influencing people by meeting their needs. However, as more and more of a person's various needs are being met elsewhere, it becomes harder and harder to motivate him.

The Problem Is People

You will probably relate to these problems:

- **Rising Inflation** With inflation soaring to the sky, operating costs are rising significantly. Energy to run things costs more; people who run things cost more. The manager today must do more with the people he or she has to work with.

- **Falling Productivity** As the inflation rate has gone up, productivity has gone down. Most organizations are actually doing less with more. Organizations are spending an overwhelming amount on ineffective systems full of ineffective people doing ineffective work.

- **Changed Employees** Managers have to cope today with a new kind of employee, a demanding cuss wanting more for doing

less. As productivity goes down, employee demands go up. And up.

- **New Kinds of Students** As the world spins faster, kids in schools are changing more and more. Some are less motivated by fear than ever before. Many are not motivated by grades. Some care more about friends or cars or drugs than anything else.

- **Challenging Children** Perhaps children are the same as they have always been— but that is no comfort to a first-time parent. Children are motivated in the same way as anyone else—but if the motivation is misapplied, they can become "spoiled" in the worst sense: their potential will be stifled.

Motivating Solutions

The solution to all of these problems lies in one approach: Motivation.

Motivators faced with these problems constantly ask themselves: **"How do I get the other person to do what I want him to do?"**

The historical answer to that question has been the whip, deftly applied. But the rack and thumbscrews are frowned upon nowadays. Black-hooded executioners are hard to find, and they don't resolve the problem anyway.

A Book of Motivation Stuff

This book will give a more modern and hopefully more effective approach to this age-old problem. Each page will give you another new idea, concept, method, or approach. The person who applies them will find others becoming more motivated to do what he or she wants them to do.

This book is only a tool box—the real solution comes when you effectively match and apply the idea to the situation.

Tried and True Advice

Follow this advice and motivation problems can be a thing of the past.

"Don't be afraid to make mistakes. If you risk little, you will probably win little. Welcome ideas from your employees. Good ideas from the rank and file are a credit to you as well as to the originator and no executive worth his salt ever feels threatened by a good idea, whatever its source.

"Always keep your promises. And don't make promises you can't keep. Never underestimate your fellow man. Good ideas can come from humble sources. Fertile minds are not always labeled with a college degree. Learn to use 'horse sense' in dealing with others. In other words, learn to treat others as you would like to be treated.

"Keep in touch with key members of your department. Don't shut yourself up in an 'ivory tower' and don't depend upon assistants to do all your leg-work for you. In controversial matters, especially, get the story yourself.

Fear, lack of trust, and absence of respect can freeze up an entire organization.

"Delegate responsibility to subordinates. By doing so, you do three things: you ease your own work load; you train deserving workers for more important posts; and you groom a competent successor who is ready to step into your shoes when it's time for you to move up the ladder or when retirement comes."

-C. G. Scholtz

A Little Fear

Fear is a powerful motivator. People are afraid that:

- you, the leader, won't trust or respect them
- they won't get that promotion
- they will be demoted
- they will lose their job
- others won't like them

But even though fear motivates powerfully, it also motivates negatively. Fear is a tool easily used that should never be used. Here are some ways people use fear:

- refusing to give praise
- making excessive demands
- continually finding fault
- ignoring with silence
- making threats
- raising the voice
- flying off the handle
- demanding that a person do precisely as told
- embarrassing someone

Despite the momentary effectiveness of fear (sometimes), over the long run it is counter-productive. Fearful people are less efficient.

Let the situation determine how much fear you use.

Their production level drops. Motivate by caring rather than by scaring. Persuasion, a challenging assignment, encouragement, sincere praise, or a pat on the back are all long-term effective motivators that will both motivate your workers and improve their morale.

16

Dirty Directions

Robert Jensen raced into the town, sweaty and late for the funeral. It was a small, hick place—but he couldn't find the mortuary. Finally he stopped to ask a boy.

"Well, sir," the boy drawled, "go to the corner where the black cow is grazing in the pasture. Turn left and go till you see a white farmhouse set in among the trees. Past that place there's an old tree that was hit by lightning. Turn right. Pretty soon you'll see a dirt road with Farmer Smith's tractor parked beside it. Go straight past it and you'll get there. If the tractor isn't there, come back and I'll give you more instructions."

Jensen never made it to the funeral. Small wonder. He was a victim of dirty directions, instructions that are so muddied or vague that they are impossible to follow.

Giving Dirty Directions

Motivators are frequently guilty of this kind of sin. And yet they wonder why their people don't perform. "He seemed to be so capable when we hired him," the manager thinks,

Look in the mirror—you might find the source of one of your main problems.

never realizing that the employee **is** capable and competent. The poor guy simply does not know what his boss wants.

The more clearly a person understands what you want, the better he can meet your expectations.

How many times have seemingly competent people disappointed you? You explained what was needed, gave all the relevant details. But then they let you down. Not only did they miss the mark, but they missed it by a mile.

"What could have gone wrong?" the boss wonders. "Halladay has such talent. He's reliable. He's everything you could want in an employee. But he is continually disappointing me!"

A Soiled Reflection

The problem, of course, is not in the stars, nor is it in the people. It may be that you are giving dirty directions. Listen carefully to yourself next time you give directions. Can the person you are talking to clearly understand?

A new father was visiting with his wife's doctor. "How long before we can have sex, Doc?"

The doctor mumbled his answer. "You'd better wait four to six weeks."

The answer was specific enough. But the communication was flawed. After thirty weeks the new father went back to the doctor. "I can't stand it anymore, Doc. Isn't there anything you can do? I just can't last the full forty-six weeks."

A Cooked Goose

Workers at the Columbus Zoo went to their supervisor for advice. "Hey, this goose keeps pecking people. What should we do?"

The supervisor was preoccupied and answered facetiously, "Feed it to the cheetahs."

Hah-hah-hah. The workers didn't know the supervisor was joking. They fed a $300 goose to the cheetahs.

Dirty Directions. They're like a plague. And your employees—or clients, or students, or children—could well be suffering from it, if their performance is continually falling short.

How Can a Motivator Correct This Situation?

Very literally, clean up his act. How? When you want someone to do something, make sure you communicate very plainly what is wanted, specifying how big, how soon, for whom, what for, how expensive.

That means you need to know exactly what you want.

If you don't know, and you're going on a fishing expedition, tell your people just that. They will kiss your feet for being honest with them.

And, by all means, don't mumble when you give instructions. Speak out. Let your voice be plain and clear. You laugh that I'm telling you something so obvious. But the new father who went without sex for thirty weeks didn't find it so funny.

Next time you give another person directions, don't tell him to look for the black cow and Farmer Smith's tractor! It's darned hard for someone to be motivated when he's not sure what you want!

Shooting Blind

There are two approaches to big-game hunting. The first is to get a clear aim on the target and squeeze the trigger very carefully. The second is to shoot blind.

When a hunter shoots blind, he fires at what he thinks is his target. Maybe he sees some movement in the bushes. "Must be a deer back there," he thinks, and fires off a shot or two.

Sometimes he gets his quarry. Sometimes it was only the wind moving the leaves. Sometimes a human casualty is the result: he hears a scream, then a moan comes from behind the bushes. A red hat rolls silently down the hill.

Some managers act like the blind leading the blind on a hunting trip—and the casualties are people!

One manager realizes there is a problem, but is not certain what it is, or how to solve it. Another manager understands the problem, but fails to communicate it. Both kinds of motivators leave their workers shooting blind at elusive objectives.

But a motivator's enthusiasm is rarely dimmed by vague targets: "We must run an efficient ship! The problem is in here somewhere. Perhaps we should improve our filing system." He shoots blind at both problem and solution. "If only Maxwell would turn out those drawings faster." The motivator shoots blind.

Human Casualties

A manager can save himself—and his workers—a lot of frustration by taking time before going hunting to think through what he wants to accomplish: consider all the possibilities of what's awry, seek outside advice, know exactly what (and where) the target is before he even picks up a gun.

When he fails to do this, there are casualties. The silent red hat.

One of my friends became such a casualty. He played a guessing game with the boss and lost. The boss didn't know exactly what he wanted, so my friend tested one solution, then another, as he desperately tried to please. Pretty soon, the boss wanted to know why this employee hadn't produced. "I am never sure exactly what you want," my friend explained.

"Small excuse!" the boss probably thought, never considering he may have been at fault.

My friend was fired.

A replacement was hired. Using him as the gun, the boss shot at some more bushes moving in the wind.

Tyranny of The Ideal

Too often, managers let The Ideal get in the way of the proper functioning of their company. They try to force-fit things so the real represents The Ideal—and in the process they destroy good things that worked very well.

Ideal	Real
Job descriptions	Real job functions
Organizational chart	The actual network
Stated intentions	Real intentions
Memos/meetings	Water cooler comments, feet-on-desk conversations
Intended communications	Real communications
Represents human activity as static	Human activity is dynamic
Taught in books and in school	Not taught but practiced

The Ideal seeks to motivate people through an artificial, contrived structure.

The real seeks to utilize the real-world structure. It is far more effective to use a structure that has naturally evolved than one you try to impose.

No-Problem Solutions

Here is an all-too-common example: A new manager came on board. He was fully briefed, informed of the company's goals, objectives, policies, told of the employees' functions, relationships, duties. He went after the job with vigor, determined to make everything work exactly according to guidelines.

Morale soon plunged to the lowest level ever. Motivation to perform had completely disappeared.

"I'm going by the book, aren't I?" the manager cried out, confused.

He was caught in the tyranny of The Ideal. The "book" explained how things were "supposed" to work—but it did not even attempt to represent the dynamics of how things actually worked, nor of how they worked best.

A wise boss suggested the new manager take two steps back and watch how the company functioned without his meddling. He soon noticed that one particular secretary was the center of things. She had a lot of real power, given her by the workers, because they trusted her and were comfortable with how she did things.

Once the manager recognized the real, instead of The Ideal, he was able to use it to motivate his workers to perform even better. He didn't seek to impose his ideal on the troops: he simply used the reality of the way the company functioned to its very best advantage.

The Ideal Club over the Head

Another manager didn't learn quite so well, and his company is still suffering from it. The Ideal was this manager's Bible, his religion, his bread and drink. When he sought to hire someone, he looked for a person who would fit the job description precisely and totally: so many years old, so much education, such and such a work background.

Since people who fit job descriptions rarely exist in the real world, he continually beat his new people over the head with what they should be.

The last time I saw him, he was still holding his job descriptions tightly to his chest, waiting for another head to bash with them.

Little did he realize that those job descriptions represented The Ideal, but not the real. "Reality" was his employees, each with unique talents and skills, who could have been very effective. But he was blind to their true abilities because he was so set on creating his Ideal.

This problem lies at the heart of all kinds of frustrations. The Ideal exists only in the mind of the Idealist. When an Ideal is stringently applied to people, whether they be workers, spouses, or children, problems will crop up. People rebel against being put into a little box—especially one that doesn't fit.

Motivation is not forcing people into an Ideal. It is being aware of and capitalizing on what is Real.

How Management Wishes Things Would Work

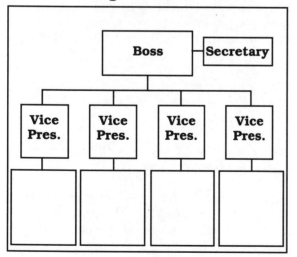

How Things Really Work

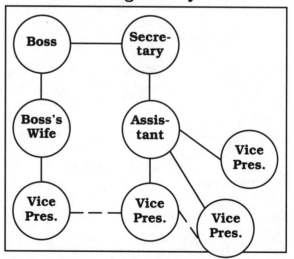

When you base your decisions on what is real, results become more effective.

It's About Time

Some people get plenty motivated to do what they're supposed to, but then fail to follow it through to completion. Why? Because they don't know how to use their time wisely.

If your workers are having trouble doing the right things, look at their use of time. **Once people learn how to manage time effectively, they're often able to motivate themselves.** And even those who aren't self-motivators will be in a better position to respond to your motivation efforts.

Some steps that will lead to more effective use of time:

• Every day, make a list of the things you need to do.

• Decide which of the tasks are most important and mark an A beside them. Mark a B beside those which need to be done, but not as soon as the first list. Mark a C beside all the others.

• Spend your time doing only A tasks, until they are all completed. Let the Bs and Cs

Those who don't control their time will find that it controls them!

remain undone until the day they move into the A category.

• If an A task is too big to do all at once, break it up into smaller tasks that can be done a little at a time.

• Promise yourself a nice reward for finishing a big project—and give it!

- Learn how to say "No" to requests that may pull you away from your highest priorities.

- Use normally wasted moments to accomplish something worthwhile.

- Learn to relax, so you are not constantly pushing yourself. When you return to your work, you will be more effective than ever before.

- Set goals to help you determine what is most important in your life.

- Keep in mind the 80/20 rule: we get 80 percent of the benefit from working on a project in the first 20 percent of the time we spend on it.

- Concentrate on only one thing at a time.

- Delegate whenever possible and appropriate.

- Group activities together—spend a block of time doing creative work, another block for phone calls, another block when you'll be open to interruptions, etc.

- Read and follow the suggestions in *How to Get Control of Your Time and Your Life*, by Alan Lakein (published by New American Library, 1974).

- Identify short-term and long-term goals you want to accomplish, and work toward them every day.

- Separate urgencies from priorities.

- Some interruptions are necessary and beneficial—some are distracting and wasteful. Welcome useful ones, eliminate wasteful ones.

- Spend 10-15 minutes every day planning and prioritizing.

- Review goals regularly.

- Eliminate floating pieces of paper. Write everything down in a permanent, easily accessible place.

- Handle a piece of paper only once.

- Take everything off your desk that you don't absolutely need at your fingertips.

- Spend time according to priority. The trivial can take care of itself, and demands only minimal time invested.

- Streamline meetings, memos, conversations. Decide the purpose, then state it, solve it, and get through with it.

- If you "might need it someday" but can't think when or why, throw it away. Be ruthless!

- Stop spending time worrying about or trying to control events that you cannot control.

- Clear off your workspace at the end of every workday.

Communicate!

One of the biggest impediments to good motivation is bad communication. The problem runs all the way from the most stately board rooms to the humblest homes: people are unable to please their motivators because they frankly don't know what's wanted.

The solution is simple. **Motivation will improve when communication improves.** When the worker knows precisely what is wanted, he or she will be able to provide it (if the demands are reasonable).

Some suggestions on communicating effectively:

• Define why you need to communicate. Decide how you want the person to respond—what do you want him to think, feel, and do as a result of the communication? Set clear objectives.

• Define exactly who the audience is. Look at your message through his or her eyes.

• Carefully choose the setting of the communication. People respond differently to

Lack of communication leaves everyone in the dark.

communications in different settings: in an office or out in the hall, over the phone or in a memo, from a podium or sitting around a table. Select the setting that will best help you accomplish your objectives.

• Select the right time for the communication. Mondays are different from Fridays for an employee. Don't try to have a heart-to-heart talk with your teenager at the very moment when he's ready to leave for a date.

• Use a variety of media and methods to communicate your ideas: charts, pictures, stories, metaphors, analogies, apperception, feelings.

• Get your listeners involved in the message. The more they are actively involved during the communication, the more they will remember.

• Use the sequence that lends itself naturally to the message.

• Concentrate on your audience's beliefs about your topic more than on the content.

• Center on the desired results of your communication more than on content.

• Answer these questions: What do I want the audience to think (or know)? Feel? Do? Make all communication decisions based on achieving these three goals.

• Packaging influences perception. Package your message in a way that your audience will perceive it favorably.

• People are drowning in information. The quicker and stronger you make your communication, the more power it will have.

• One well-stated, tight message is worth twenty muddied, vague messages.

• Narrow your target audience. The broader your audience, the weaker the message.

• Retention is the key. If they don't remember it, it didn't work.

• Simple = effective

• The biggest communication failure happens when the audience doesn't see what you are talking about.

• When you show the audience the value of your message in their life, retention and application of your ideas increases.

• The ultimate test of effectiveness is this: did they adopt your message as their own.

Pawn or Person?

People like to have some control over their destinies. They like to feel they are more than a pawn in someone else's game. Because of this, people commonly make suggestions to their leaders. "Have we ever tried this approach?" "Why don't we do the job this way—it seems to me it would work better."

Some of those suggestions can make a real difference to the company or group. They may mark a turning point in production or they may be absolutely useless, but they are worth a try. The people down on the line, fighting the daily fight with their jobs, can often see the real problems better than their leaders can. They can also see solutions that may never occur to the leader.

Leaders who establish a climate that is conducive to suggestions are ultimately more effective. And their people are more effective—they feel more responsibility for what they are doing, and respond accordingly.

The leader doesn't have to follow all the suggestions he or she receives, but each suggestion should be treated with respect.

People are not pawns for someone else to move about at will.

Some suggestions for dealing with suggestions in ways that will motivate:

• Listen carefully when someone makes a suggestion. Make sure you understand exactly what's being said.

• Never turn down an idea on the spot. Tell the other person you would like to think it over—even if you know the idea is a real dog. People often think about something for quite a while before they ever say anything to their leader. They deserve the courtesy of having their leader think about the idea (or sit on it) for a while. They also merit the courtesy of a response.

• Occasionally discuss the ideas with someone else. That will show the person you value his idea enough to take it to another person for input.

• Show appreciation to the person for caring enough to make the suggestion.

• If you have to turn the idea down, reject it gently, explaining the reason.

• Whenever you can, ask for suggestions from your workers on how to deal with specific problems.

Sometimes the games must stop and you realize you are dealing with real people.

Performance Ceiling

Production always goes down when a preset maximum level of performance is reached. A maximum limits the person's potential. Instead of being a goal to reach for, it becomes a barrier to resist.

Subliminal and Understood Limits

Of course, nearly everyone says, "The sky's the limit." But there's a discrepancy between that stated attitude and the real attitude that most people perceive. The superperformer is often threatening to others, his peers and bosses alike. So he may be encouraged to conform to the lesser performance of the others.

- A secretary gets fired. The argument: "She's uppity." But the real reason is that she went past the ceiling her boss had set. She had too many good ideas for improving the company. (The problem was that her ideas really were good. If her ideas had been mediocre, her boss would not have worried.)

- A union worker gets in trouble because his production is so high. The union officials

A ceiling can be an impossible dream, a raised banner, a large club, or a goal to be reached.

pull him to the side, "Slow down. You're doing too much. It makes the others look bad."

- A teacher in Maryland gets suspended for teaching his students too much. The course was on Shakespeare—and he

29

threw in a little Aristotle for good measure. The problem: he exceeded the ceiling his school board had set, since all the curriculum was supposed to be standard. It didn't matter that his students were more excited—and getting a better education—than anyone else in the school.

• A certain man was an alcoholic. His wife begged, pleaded, nagged, cried. "Please quit; won't you please, please quit?" But deep down inside she wanted him to continue drinking—she needed to feel needed! He was dependent on his booze and she was dependent on taking care of him when he was drunk. She unconsciously created a performance ceiling for him by needing him to continue drinking.

• A new manager of a medical supply house begins to call in his area supervisors for weekly meetings. They have lunch together; the meetings start to mold the group more into a club than a company. Everyone recognizes that the meetings are nonproductive, but they can't quit. They're having so much fun that they put a ceiling on their performance by choosing not to perform.

• A child has a great potential to become a loving effective human being. But at home, all he sees is bickering and fault-finding. His mom constantly criticizes his dad, who slouches into his favorite chair and does little more than read the newspaper. The child could learn better—but he probably won't. His environment is putting a ceiling on his performance.

Ceilings

Think what ceilings do for you. It feels comfortable to have a ceiling up there. You feel protected and safe. Some people may feel that the ceiling gives them something to reach for, to stretch for. But more often it's a limitation, a restriction.

If there's ever been an organization that didn't have a ceiling of some form, I've never heard of it. Such organizations just don't exist. The ceiling is usually never stated, never recorded, never made official—but it's there just the same.

The performance ceiling grows out of a company's self-image. It is created by how management views itself and the company's potential. The boss, his key people, the workers on every level, their families, unions, outside economic conditions—they all contribute to the performance ceiling of a company. Their fears and insecurities gradually build up limits to what the company can do. Before they know it, they have created a very real roof above their heads.

A performance ceiling in the classroom can grow out of a teacher's expectations. He may figure that all kids are only half-smart, and give out assignments accordingly. Or he may divide the class into groups: smart, half-smart, and no-smarts. The smart kids' ceiling will be very high (and they probably will lack some good competition)—but the half-smarts and no-smarts will have respectively lower ceilings holding them down. Try

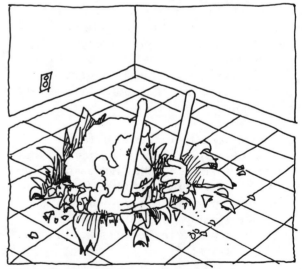

A manager can help employees break through the performance ceiling. Then the process starts anew.

as they might, they won't be able to progress past the point of the teacher's expectations.

How do you cope with this subliminal ceiling?

First, realize that change is a slow process. A ceiling isn't erected all at once, and it cannot be torn down all at once.

Second, learn precisely where the ceiling sits above your head. State clearly what the problem is.

Third, create a situation that conflicts with the ceiling. Perhaps you can find evidence showing that the "tried-and-true" ways aren't working. Perhaps you can motivate a person or group to have success beyond the level normally allowed by the ceiling. Your evidence of better performance can show that the ceiling is an illusion, that it can be surpassed.

Fourth, even when you move slowly, you must be sure to take it a step at a time. Move in progressive stages, raising the performance ceiling a little bit at a time, methodically making it ever a little higher and higher.

Charles Schwab, one of Andrew Carnegie's right-hand men, showed how a performance ceiling can be raised. One day he was called in to help with a mill that had atrocious production. The mill manager had "tried every trick in the book" to raise the level of production, but nothing worked.

Schwab thought about the problem for a moment, then with a piece of chalk wrote a huge six on the floor. Then he left.

When the night shift came in they saw the number on the floor. "What's that for?" they asked.
"Oh, that's how many heats we can make in a day," the day-shift men replied.

"Oh, yeah?" the night-shift men said. "We can top that!" The next morning when the day shift came they looked at the floor. The chalked-in six had been wiped out and in its place was a seven. The day-shift men weren't going to be outdone. They worked as they had never worked before. At the end of the day they chalked in an incredible ten.

Production continued to rise as never before. The secret, of course, was simple: raise the performance level, little by little. As the ceiling rises, performance will climb right with it.

Minimax

Minimax. **It means to minimize weaknesses and maximize strengths.**

The more you're able to minimize weaknesses, the stronger your group will become. If, in addition, you're able to maximize strengths, your people will be incredibly motivated.

Minimax is a valuable motivational tool. The person who uses it is able to get the most out of those he works with.

Every worker in the world has weaknesses. Students have weaknesses. Sales prospects have them. Children have them.

The reason why companies hire one person over another is that the winning candidate has some notable strengths. And how did he get them? By emphasizing key aspects of his personality and downplaying others.

You can settle for the worker who doesn't have any great weaknesses. But—sorry—

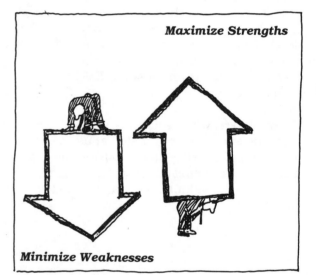

Maximize Strengths

Minimize Weaknesses

that same person won't have any great strengths, either. There's a word for that kind of employee: mediocre. If that's what you want, welcome to it.

But if you want the strengths, you've got to be ready for weaknesses too. Wherever there are mountains you also find valleys.

How do you utilize minimax? There are two steps:

Step 1: Avoid Emphasizing Weaknesses.

If you spend time trying to correct a lot of weaknesses, you may end up with just a lot of wasted time. And if you look for weaknesses to avoid when hiring, you will probably end up with mediocrity.

Emphasis on weakness destroys morale—and it can destroy your entire operation.

I know a research engineer who worked for a major company. He was outstanding in his work, one of the most brilliant in his field. But he had a weakness, and his managers chose to emphasize it: he was a sloppy dresser.

His department was an area of pride to management. When visitors came, they always took them through the research lab. It had made some vital contributions to science, and the lab was very interesting to tour.

But there in the middle of the lab was this sloppy engineer. The managers grew increasingly embarrassed. They concentrated on the weakness and began to apply more and more pressure on the engineer to conform to their standard of neatness.

Soon, dress standards became an obsession, and management's harassment was annoying and distracting. The engineer was enticed away to a competing company that concentrated on strengths more than on weaknesses.

The engineer's previous employer is still paying for that mistake.

This problem is not restricted to business alone. Look back at your school experience. Chances are that your strengths were ignored and your weaknesses emphasized. A child may be great in math but weak in

reading. So where is all the emphasis placed? That's right—on the reading. He ends up feeling like a failure because of the reading, and he never has the chance to grow in math.

Step 2: Build on Strength.

It's not enough to avoid emphasizing weakness. It may make the employee glad you're off his back—but it won't help him grow. So you build on his strengths. Learn what he does best, and then help him do it better.

When you hired your employee, there was something outstanding about him, something that made you say to yourself, This one can really do the job! Always keep that initial enthusiasm in mind. What job was it you knew he could do? Answer that question and you've got a good lead on his main strength. Now build on it.

If the engineer's employers had applied Minimax, they would not still be suffering the loss of their most talented researcher. They should have spent more time nurturing his genius than punishing his idiosyncrasy. For example, if their emphasis had been on performance, they may have let him work during his most productive hours, instead of the company's artificial work schedule; gotten him the kind of assistants he needed; made sure he had the equipment he needed; let him attend conferences and seminars; bought for him the best journals and research publications—these are all examples of building on strength.

The child in school should learn to read, of course. But if he's a whiz at math, the teacher can use that ability to help him in other courses. When the teacher builds on the student's strength in math, the student will feel better about himself. He'll improve in math. And, as his self-esteem grows, he'll be more willing to tackle the problem of reading.

Another way the teacher can build on the student's strength in math is to use math to open the reading door. Consider the typical math problem:

"Farmer Brown had seven chickens, and four of the chickens laid an egg every other day. One of the chickens laid an egg every day. Two of the chickens laid an egg only once a week. How many eggs did Farmer Brown have at the end of each week?"

Usually, students will use their reading ability to figure out just what the question is asking. But a student who is good in math can take the opposite approach—he can use the numerical information to help him decipher what he needs to know. That's building on strength in its finest form. That's minimizing weaknesses and maximizing strengths.

The Japanese have shown us the way with minimax. It's well known that Japanese production is considered some of the best in the world. For a Japanese person, his company is his life. He's married to it. Divorce from the company is virtually unheard of.

In that setting, Japanese managers must make the very best of each worker. They

Some managers do all they can to capitalize on weakness, not strength. It's like giving a football to a basketball player, like telling your star fullback to play forward.

don't consider firing him or having him quit as viable alternatives. If they want to get the job done, they've got to focus on strength.

As some Japanese executives mentioned to Peter Drucker, "The less we know about his weaknesses, the better. What we need to know are the strengths of a man and what he can do."

Stuck

Sometimes a highly motivated person gets stuck on a problem and ceases to perform. To all outward appearances, he's lost his motivation, and he needs something to get him going again. But sometimes motivation isn't really what's needed. Instead, the person needs assistance in creative problem-solving.

It's literally impossible to motivate a person to get going when he's creatively stuck. Instead, provide him with some help in solving the problem, and then he'll motivate himself.

Some ways to creatively solve problems:

• Ask key questions about the problem: Who? What? When? Where? Why? Which? How? How much?

• Get a group together and brainstorm.

• Look at similar situations in nature, and see how Mother Nature solved the problem. (By using this approach, the hypodermic needle was patterned after the

When your brain is running at half speed, it's hard to get motivated about anything.

rattlesnake fang, the camera was patterned after the human eye, the submarine was patterned after the fish.)

• Use metamorphosis—see yourself as the problem, and figure out the solution from that point of view.

• Ask a *real* expert. But watch out! Some people like to talk about solving similar problems, but haven't ever done it. Find the people who have actually tackled similar problems.

• Strip the problem back to its essence, to be sure you're defining it correctly. (The problem on a busy street is not how to improve the speed bumps, but how to slow the cars down. Or how to keep them off the street completely!)

• Pass it off to someone else. Who said you are the best one for the problem? A big ego may actually blind you to a certain path for a solution. Another path and another person may be the best solution.

• Play the "What If?" Game: What if this were the solution? or, What if that were the solution?

• Put your subconscious to work for you. It has great capabilities that are often untapped. To use the subconscious:

1. Study the problem and try to resolve it.

2. If an answer won't come, tell your subconscious mind to get to work on it—and then forget it.

3. When you need the solution, think about it consciously again. The subconscious will give you input you hadn't thought of.

4. Write down the answer when it comes. At first, it may not make a lot of sense—but give it a chance.

Why Is Play Fun?

Most people work so they can play. They dread their eight-to-five existence, but they put up with it so they can have money to survive—and money to have fun after work.

If you look hard enough, though, you'll find that rare bird who's the exception. He can't wait to get to work. He dreads leaving at night.

How can this be? Surely everyone would rather have fun than work!

The answer becomes apparent when we take a good look at our rare bird: he loves his work because it's fun for him.

You know your employees have the potential to work together. Watch them in their bowling league. They're unified, cohesive, successful. At work they're at odds with each other. But when they're playing they have all the attributes you wish they'd have at work.

Here's the secret: if you want to motivate your people, make their work fun! Apply to work the elements that make games enjoyable.

If you want to motivate people in any group to do something, make it fun for them. Let's say your group needs to do a fund raiser—it can be approached in one of two ways. You can prepare them for the drudgery and hassle of raising money. Or you can pep them up for a fun time. Which approach do you think will work best?

The house needs to be cleaned and the kids won't pitch in and help? Make a game of it, and it will be spick-and-span before you know it! A friend of mine motivated her younger sisters to clean house by playing robots. Each robot had a timed amount to accomplish several jobs. Every three to five minutes, the timer would ring, and the robots would report back to her what they had accomplished. An hour of housework flew by and they all loved it.

Students in a class moan and groan every time they get an assignment? Turn the assignment into a game, complete with rules and rewards. Then watch them work like never before because they're having fun!

Can Monopoly, golf, and football be applied to the corporation? You bet your blue chips they can!

Unified Play Is Fun Because:

- All players share the same clear, visible objective.
- All players have only one prime goal.
- The rules are clear and simple and are understood by all.
- The objective is challenging but obtainable.
- All players receive immediate and continual feedback on how they are doing.
- The game often involves a team in which each member is recognized as a needed part.
- The game involves a wide variety of senses and skills.

- Progress and results are objectively recorded for all to see and compare.
- The emphasis is on results and enjoying the process that brings them.

Some Fun Sometime

Workers gravitate to their types of jobs because initially they enjoy them. Then something happens. Someone, probably a manager, says, "Hey, work shouldn't be fun. Work should be **work**! If the workers are having fun, that means that they aren't being as productive as they could be. Fun violates the Puritan ethic!"

So the manager sets down rules and regulations and policies that methodically destroy the spirit of his workers. And, before too long, they have stopped enjoying their jobs and are only enduring them.
The paradox is that people generally get a heck of a lot more done when they're having at least some fun than when work is a drudgery. Make work fun for your workers— and they'll really be motivated to work!

A Matter of Habit

Ninety-nine percent of everything we do is habit. Give or take a percent. Competence is a matter of habit. Concentration is a matter of habit. Effectiveness, confidence, positive attitude, even habit is a matter of habit!

Much of motivation involves changing someone's habits. Here's a key: to change someone's habit pattern, you have to substitute a better habit pattern.

Provide a Better Route

If you fill in someone's rut, be sure you give him another route to take.

Too often people are ordered to change their old patterns, without an alternate approach. If you want people to change, show them the better way you want them to go. If you don't, they'll only see a threat—and they'll positively balk (and snort!) at your proposed changes.

But you need to do more than give them a better alternative: they need to see that it's

Filling in ruts stops progress and kills innovation. Instead of making them work on old roads, give your people a new road to take.

better. People are usually quite comfortable with their established patterns and routines. So when you go about changing them, you need to show them that your approach will be even better for them.

Causing a Flood

Changing habits is like changing the flow of a stream of water. First the stream is going along in its own path and doing fine. Then someone comes along and dams up the stream. If no alternate path is provided, a horrible flood will result.

And after the flood? The stream continues in the same path it was in initially.

Lemon-Drop Substitution

When you want to motivate a change in someone's habits, think of him or her as a cigarette smoker. A smoker won't change his habit unless he can see the benefit in changing. And it has to be a benefit from his own point of view, not someone else's. You can tell a man all day long that smoking is bad for his health, but until he perceives your warnings as relevant for him, he'll never change.

But suppose a smoker does get motivated to change his habit. What then? He'll probably be unsuccessful unless he finds a substitute for his cigarettes. Maybe he starts to chew gum; maybe he sucks on lemon drops. Whatever he chooses, it's vital that he have something he now does instead of smoking. If he were to simply stop, without making a substitute of some kind, he'd be creating a vacuum. Nature hates vacuums; it rushes to fill them in.

Gung-ho Joe

Not too long ago a manufacturer was worried about the efficiency of one of his main assembly lines. The workers had set patterns over the years, haphazardly establishing their method of work. It was indeed inefficient.

So the manufacturer hired a new manager to straighten things up. The manager went to work with a will. "Gung-ho" would understate his enthusiasm. He proceeded to rearrange the physical plant, changing the work flow to increase productivity.

And the productivity promptly dropped to an all-time low.

Why? Because the manager was messing with their habit patterns. He made a change without convincing the workers that it was for the better, that it would be to their advantage. So the workers "got back" at him, even to the point of sabotaging the plant.

Recipe for Change

There are two ingredients to motivating a change of habit—and remember that both ingredients must be present to make the change effective:

1. Substitute a new, more desirable pattern.

2. Convince those involved that the new pattern is indeed better both for the individual and for the group.

The Distance Factor

The farther you get from your people, in terms of organizational structure, the less effective you'll be. As the organizational chart grows taller, communication gets more and more difficult, as does motivation. The following example illustrates:

The Colonel Told the Major—At nine o'clock tomorrow there will be an eclipse of the sun, something which does not occur every day. Get the men to fall out in the company street in their fatigues so that they will see this rare phenomenon, and I will explain it to them. In case of rain, we will not be able to see anything, so take the men to the gym.

The Major Told the Captain—By order of the Colonel, tomorrow at nine o'clock there will be an eclipse of the sun. If it rains you will not be able to see it from the company street, so then, in fatigues, the eclipse of the sun will take place in the gym, something that does not occur every day.

The Captain Told the Lieutenant—By order of the Colonel in fatigues tomorrow at nine o'clock in the morning the inauguration of the eclipse of the sun will take place in the gym. The Colonel will give the order if it should rain in the company street, something which occurs every day.

The Lieutenant Told the Sergeant—Tomorrow at nine the Colonel in fatigues will eclipse the sun in the gym, as it occurs every day if it is a nice day. If it rains, then in the company street.

The Sergeant Told the Corporal—Tomorrow at nine the eclipse of the Colonel in fatigues will take place by cause of the sun. If it rains in the gym, something which does not take place every day, you will fall out in the company street.

What the Privates Understood—Tomorrow, if it rains, it looks as if the sun will eclipse the Colonel in the gym. It is a shame that this does not occur every day.

—Author Unknown

Criticism on a Bun

It is better to give than receive—and that goes for criticism as well as anything else. Everyone I know, bar none, would much rather give it than get it.

If criticism is handled right, however, it can be motivational rather than discouraging. The time invariably comes when a motivator must point out problems in his or her people. It's easy for a person to get into wrong habits without even realizing it—we're often too close to our own problems to see what they are. In such cases, the motivator must give feedback, point out what's wrong, tell the other person what he needs to do to change.

How does the manager make it motivational? **Whenever you give criticism, be sure to sandwich it in between positive comments about the person's work.**

Sometimes it might be hard to find positive things to say about a particular person. But if you try you'll find a way!

Be Honest
A key in giving praise is to be honest. If the boss or parent or teacher gives praise deceptively, he'll be found out. And that will be worse than any criticism ever given.

Be Clear
State the problem exactly. If you can't put it into words, don't even bring it up.

Be Open
You've got to be willing to take it as well as give it. The best motivators are the ones who let their people offer polite criticism to them.

\+ Good point

\- Criticism

\+ Good point

The Little Things

Motivators have been tried and convicted. They have been found guilty of looking beyond the mark and ignoring the little things.

"Smith is dissatisfied? Well, give her a raise. She'll change her tune real quick."

People in the motivation business (and that includes every manager on every level on the face of the earth) seem to collectively believe two false myths: everyone has a price, and that price can be met with money.

- If your people seem to be unhappy, you give them more money.

- If you want to increase productivity, you hold out a carrot of more money.

- If they threaten to leave for a better job, you raise their salary.

Money seems to be viewed as the universal cure-all, Doctor Proctor's Magical Secret Golden Elixir That Will Solve All Your Work Problems.

If you want to hit the mark, you need to know where the target is.

Money is used on kids as well as workers:

- "Do your chores and I'll give you extra allowance."

- "Don't waste that food—it costs money!"

- "You'd better do well in school if you want to get a good-paying job when you grow up."

But often money is a poor motivator, especially if other problems exist. There are many "little" things that motivate much better.

Better Motivators

When your workers talk to people who really care about them, their spouses or close friends, they reveal what really motivates them. It's usually the little things, the things that are missing. But those things really aren't so little when you don't have them. Consider these:

"I'd be happier at work if only the boss would express a little appreciation."

"I think I'd do better at work if I only felt that what I did made a difference."

"The trouble with my job is that it's all the same. It was challenging until I got the hang of it; now it's just a bore."

"My folks buy me everything I want. But I wish they'd give me a little of their time."

"I'd be happy to help around the house if only I felt someone really cared."

The "little things." Self-worth. Growth. Credit. Freedom. Confidence and trust. Those are the things that motivate people. Find out what they need and then give it to them.

Reaching for your wallet is not always the answer. Try stretching out your hand or speaking a few encouraging words to find motivation techniques that work.

Everybody's Weak Spot

Most people are fearfully insecure. And that's not just my opinion. A well-known psychologist recently stated that "75 percent of corporation employees, including a lot of presidents and vice-presidents, are very anxious, fearful people by nature and fundamentally insecure.... I can't tell you the number of companies I've seen composed of cringing wretches."

Do you have some people who are, by nature, cringing wretches? If so, you have a great opportunity to help a fellow human in need. And at the same time you can motivate and inspire them to better and brighter performance in your company.

You know the story of Achilles: his entire body was invulnerable except one small part. That weak spot became his downfall.

Everyone on earth has a weak spot. Usually it's insecurity that makes a person weakest of all.

If you can help protect and strengthen people where they feel weak, they will become dependent upon you.

The biggest weakness of most workers is insecurity. They are constantly afraid that they will blow it and lose everything.

Security from Another

The insecure person fears how he looks to others. Tell him "You're doing a great job: you're going strong."

The insecure person is worried that he might flub up and lose his job. Tell him: "I hope you know how much we appreciate you here. I don't know what we'd do if you weren't working here."

The insecure person lacks confidence in his work. You can give him confidence by helping him gradually gain competence in new levels of work, progressively enabling him to have success in new areas.

Help an insecure person become secure and he'll be dependent on you. But that can have its negative side. He can suck your resources away. He can put a lot of pressure on you until you know that if you fail, he'll fail too.

Leaning on Strength

If the other people on your team forever lean on you, they'll never develop their own strength. I remember tying a pipe to a young sapling to help it stand up. The pipe made all the difference. One day the tree was ready to fall over and die; the next day, it was standing straight, aided by the pipe. Finally I thought the tree was ready to stand alone, and I removed the pipe.
Bad guess! The first strong wind blew it over.

Leaning doesn't produce strength. But it's often the only place you can start. Help your people feel more secure. Support them, while letting them stand on their own. Gradually help them learn to have a feeling of confidence in themselves. In time the result will be confident members on a competent team. That's Motivation with a capital M.

The 3 C's

The key to being a good motivator is being a good leader. The leader can push and force and shout and threaten, and he may get the job done for a while. But his people aren't really motivated—they're just trying to stay out of his way. In the end, he will lose them.

It's much better to try to draw people after you than to try to push them. H.W. Prisits, Jr., identifies three major qualities of a good leader:

"To be a real leader, a person must observe what I call the 'Three C's of Leadership.'

"The first C: he will make as many problems as possible a matter of common council. People will always cooperate in carrying out a policy if they feel they have had a voice in making it. 'Our plan' is always better than 'my plan.'

"The next C is courteous consideration. More than a ready smile and convenient politeness, courteous consideration is the willingness of an executive to give of his personal time when it is not convenient. It is his capacity to give an understanding and patient hearing to the ideas of subordinates, and to offer encouragement and counsel when it is needed—not just when it is easy to give.

"The Final C is to concede credit. Nothing costs an executive so little and nothing can provide greater pleasure or bring closer cooperation than to give the other fellow credit for something he has done well."

What Makes a Poor Leader?

What kind of people don't make good leaders or motivators? A study by a team of psychologists at the University of California found them to be:

- **Aggressive** against people who do not agree with them, or who do not do as they want them to.

- **Apprehensive** that others are scheming against them or the firm.

- **Fatalistic** in thinking that most workers aren't to be trusted; intolerant of democratic leaders.

- **Inflexible**, believing that there must be no deviation from the course they have set.

- **Impulsive**, preferring action to thinking it over before acting.

- **Prejudiced** against certain social groups, firms, religions, or nations.

- **Submissive** in blindly believing in, and following, forceful leaders or achievers whom they admire.

From *Bits and Pieces*

A Fairy Tale

Once upon a time, in a land far away, the people lived in darkness both day and night. Every day they would sit in the same spot alone and unaware, not knowing they could move, not knowing the world was broad and wide.

Then the Creature came to them. He had sixteen hands and was very powerful. With his hands he had learned to move about— and he taught the people how to move. At first they were fearful, but gradually they left their solitary spots and began to spread across the land. It was a time of great joy.

With their hands the people learned to "see" their way to any place they wished to visit. With their hands they learned to build houses to live in: they learned how to sow the land with seeds to give them more and better food.

The Creature became their hero. They honored and worshipped him for all he had done for them. They loved the Creature, and he loved his people. Then one day the Creature discovered Light. It brought glorious vision.

He was overwhelmed. "This will bring immeasurable joy into the hearts of my people," he thought. And he brought the Light to the people.

At first they were afraid, but then, one by one, they faced the Light the Creature held in his hand.

"He is so ugly," one whispered.

"The Creature has sixteen hands," said another. "He is a freak. "

"Is this the being we thought was wonderful?" asked a third. "He has surely deceived us!"

Then, as one man, the people attacked the Ugly Creature with Sixteen Hands. They took the Light from him and drove him out of their land.

The Creature found a hiding place and wept. He thought of all the things he could have brought the people. He thought of all the things he could have done to make their lives *better: the warmth of the sun, the gentle breezes of the wind, the wonder of the rainbow.*

But the people wouldn't have it. With the Creature gone they rejoiced at their glorious victory over such a vile beast. "He nearly deceived us," they said, greatly relieved. "Lucky we saw him in the Light, to realize what he really is."

With that, all the people of the land began to dance and sing in joy. It was a wonderful celebration. But the people became so caught up in their reveling that they didn't notice the Light slowly growing dimmer and dimmer. They didn't see it at all—until the Light was totally gone.

In darkness once again, the people used their hands to feel their way back to their homes.

We love the inventions, creations, and innovations, but we can't stand the inventors, creators, and innovators. They often work in apparent chaos, we don't understand their ways—and if there is one thing organizations crave it is order and predictability. Yet, in order to be creative, innovators must break away from established ways and norms.

We love the fruit, but we don't like the tree it comes from.

The natural tendency of any organization is to rid itself of the chaotic and unpredictable; yet, the very presence of creative and innovative people was what brought the company about in the first place. Without them there is no progress, no growth, no balance.

Committees

A major war is being waged nowadays over what committees are for and how they can most effectively be motivated and used. Management is most often the loser.

Committees are often used as a device for:

• making decisions

• creating new ideas

• effectively evaluating

They are good at none of those things. The manager who tries to motivate a committee to do those kinds of things effectively is only asking for trouble.

Committees are more effective for:

• generating alternatives

• hammering out compromises

• extending debate past lunch break

The usual method of motivating committees consists of applying pressure to do the impossible. The largest problem is that the manager has created a thing that cannot do what's being asked.

Committee Motivation

Most organizations spend 7 to 15 percent of their personnel budgets (and personnel time) on committees.

The manager finds himself losing sleep and getting ulcers because things aren't going as well as he would like. "How can I motivate that committee to do better?" he asks himself, tossing and turning in his bed.

The answer is simple: give the committee a task it can accomplish.

You wouldn't give a herd of elephants the job of plucking a chicken. Why would you give a committee the job of making decisions or recommendations for your company?

Same Output, Different Size

I'm familiar with two publishers whose output is remarkably similar. An outsider comparing their production would probably conclude that their staffs were about the same size. But they aren't even close. One has 60 full- and part-time workers—and the other has only 7!

What makes the difference? The larger organization is run by committees.

In the larger organization more time is spent talking about work than actually doing it. The entire staff suffers under the concept that more is better, that a crowd can solve a problem better than any single individual.

As usual, Peter Drucker hits the nail on the head: *"My first grade arithmetic primer asked: 'If it takes two ditch-diggers two days to dig a ditch, how long would it take four ditch-diggers?' In first grade, the correct answer is, of course, 'one day.' In the kind of work, however, with which executives are concerned, the right answer is probably 'four days' if not 'forever.'"*

Too many cooks spoil the broth, but the cooks will praise one another on how it could never have been done without everyone's constructive output.

The World's Only Monument To A Committee

Herzberg's Two-Factor Theory

Frederick Herzberg is a behavioral scientist who has seen people and their relationships to their jobs in a new way. He has done extensive studies, asking his subjects to think of times when they felt particularly good or particularly bad about their jobs.

Herzberg learned that money is not a prime motivator in getting people to do better work—although it may be very important as a means of getting things that do motivate, such as prestige and recognition. He learned that security is not a prime motivator either, nor is a bright, cheery atmosphere in the workplace.

In his final analysis, Herzberg showed that every manager has two different kinds of factors he must consider in dealing with his workers: motivation and maintenance. Both kinds are absolutely necessary in getting the job done, and although they must be considered separately, the factors are not directly linked.

Motivation Factors

The presence of motivation factors will both satisfy and motivate employees. Though their absence may not necessarily cause dissatisfaction, it will decrease motivation. The factors:

- **Achievement:** The worker needs to feel that he has accomplished something.

- **Recognition:** The worker needs to feel that his achievement has been noticed.

- **Interesting duties:** The worker needs to feel interest in the work itself.

- **Responsibility:** The worker needs to feel that he is responsible for himself and for his own work. Responsibility for new tasks and duties is also important.

- **Opportunity for growth:** The worker needs to feel that he has the potential to grow within the organization.

Maintenance Factors

These factors simply keep the worker on the job—they keep him or her from going elsewhere for work. The presence of these factors causes satisfaction; their absence causes dissatisfaction. Their presence or absence has no effect, however, on motivation. The factors:

- **Supervision:** The worker feels that the manager is willing to teach and delegate responsibility.

- **Administration:** The worker feels that management has good communication with the worker. Also, the worker feels good about company and personnel policies.

- **Working conditions:** The worker feels good about the physical conditions at work.

- **Interrelationships:** The worker feels good about his relations with peers, subordinates, and superiors.

- **Status:** The worker feels that his job has status and rank.

- **Security:** The worker feels secure about his job.

- **Salary:** The worker feels adequately compensated for his work.

- **Personal life:** The worker feels that the job (hours, transfers, etc.) does not adversely affect his personal life.

Maintenance factors must be met to keep the worker doing the job. Motivating factors will get the worker to do the work better. The wise manager will use both factors to effectively maintain and improve worker satisfaction and performance.

The Other Guy's Opinion

Seeing another's point of view is often crucial to establishing a good working relationship. To help you see what the other guy is thinking, I've collected a few comments from both management and workers, both parents and children, both teachers and students.

What the Bosses Are Saying about Their Workers

• Can't anyone ever take any initiative?

• It seems like my workers don't care beans about the kind of job they do.

• What's the use of trying—you can't satisfy this staff no matter what you do.

• When you ask for feedback, all they do is complain—so why even ask?

• Here's my method: just tell them what I want and demand that I get it.

• If you give them an inch, they'll take a mile.

• Why can't they grow up? I don't have time to handle all their personal problems.

• I'm sick of listening to their petty complaints.

• They want to get ahead, but they're not willing to learn more about the company and make themselves more valuable.

• We have a meeting and I lay the law down to them. Then they go right out and do their own thing.

• I tell them exactly how I want a job done— but somehow they always screw up.

• Why do they have to wait until there is a crisis before they tell me they can't handle a job? If they'd be up-front about it, I could find another solution.

• If only I could get some decent help. If only I could find someone who cared about the company instead of themselves.

- Nobody knows anything. You would think they might know how to dress, how to talk to people—but they don't.

- I want someone who can handle a problem when it comes up, not someone who is going to run to me for every little decision.

- Why do they take things into their own hands instead of asking me how I would like it handled?

- Why doesn't anyone ever stick around? I just get them trained and then they move on.

- They just don't realize how lucky they are to work here.

- I pay them a good salary—what else do they want?

- Our policy is the way it is. If they don't like it they can always leave.

- I don't want all these workers bothering me. I have important things to do.

- I'm always available to the staff, but they rarely come in and talk to me.

- I guess we're going to have to have a training meeting and tell them our procedures one more time.

What Workers Are Saying about Their Bosses

- They don't understand our problems.

- They sit in their nice offices, just sitting around talking while we do all the work. They don't care about me. I'm just a number to them.

- I wish they would listen to my idea. They don't know how to run this place.

- How can they be so stupid?

- She tells me she'll be back at 1:00 and then she doesn't show up until 3:00. I'm trying to explain to her appointments where she is. She makes me look like a fool.

- He never gives me enough authority to get the job done.

- If they would tell me what's going on, I would know what to tell the customers.

- He says one thing today and then tomorrow he says something totally different.

- They lie to the customer and don't tell me—I'm left with a big hunk of egg on my face.

- They don't listen to my problems. I'm convinced they couldn't care less.

- I put in my eight hours, do what I have to do to keep my job. And then I'm out of there.

- I just try not to rock the boat or to cause any trouble.

- If they would tell me what they expect from me, I could do it.

- Oh-oh—another meeting. I wonder what we're doing wrong now.

- If she had to do my job for even five minutes, she'd quit!

- The system is so inefficient. I could tell him how to make it work, but he wouldn't listen anyway.

- Employees aren't people. Management thinks they could replace you in a minute. But I'm convinced no one is expendable. They're so goofed up. They don't know what's what. How he got to be where he is now, I'll never know!

- He used to be a good guy. Then they promoted him.

- How do you get into the ivory tower to talk? He sits up there with no contact with the real world.

- They think they can give me a title and that will make me happy.

- They gave me a lousy $50 a month raise, but I know how much they're making.

- I make one mistake and they're ready to fire me.

- They gave me this job and I don't have the foggiest idea how to do it. But if I ask for help, they'll call me incompetent.

- She expects me to read her mind.

- Why don't they get some decent equipment? It would save hours.

- I'm ten minutes late for work one day and they're down on me for a month.

- I can't answer the customers' questions because I don't know myself.

- How come he doesn't do any work? I'll bet he doesn't work three hours a day.

- Another awful office party. Why can't they ever do anything fun?

- They are exempt from obeying the silly rules that we could get fired for breaking.

What Children Are Saying about Their Parents

- Let me live my own life.

- Let me spend my money the way I want.

- How do you know what I want?

- Lecture. Lecture. Lecture.

- I would love to help, but you never ask.

- Why is your way better than mine?

- You're always mad at me and I don't know why.

- What difference does it make if my room is dirty? Why can't I sleep in; who does it hurt?

- I don't want to help grandpa—why don't you do it?

- You're always trying to impress the neighbors; who cares what they think?

- You buy whatever you want, but you never have any money to give to me.

- Why do I have to go to bed when you can stay up?

- Why do I have to wash my face?

- How come we always watch the TV show you want to see?

- You never like any of my friends.

- Why do you criticize my driving when I'm a lot better than you are?

- I always have to do the crummy jobs that you don't like to do.

- All you do is talk on the phone to your friends.

- My dad never has time for me, but he always manages to play golf with his friends.

- Don't you ever think about anything except work?

- I'll bet your grades weren't any better than mine, but you act like I'm a criminal if I get a C!

- You don't understand.

- All you want to do is gossip with your friends.

- You don't really care about people; it's just for show.

- Don't you trust me?

- My parents are so nosy, they want to know what I'm doing, who I'm with, when I will be home. It drives me crazy!

- Quit treating me like a child!

- You don't think I can take care of myself.

- You always tell me what I'm doing wrong. Why don't you tell me about all the good things I do?

What Parents Are Saying about Their Children

- Every time I give them a job to do they take all day to do it and then they don't do it right.

- He always has energy to play with his friends, but taking the garbage out is just too much work.

- He is really smart, but he just doesn't apply himself to his homework.

- I don't know where they find their friends.

- Just when I think she is a disaster, she does something wonderful that blows my mind. She is so smart it scares me!

- Why won't they learn from my experiences?

- He would sleep till noon if I would let him. What is the big deal about cleaning a bedroom?

- You would think that after I have prepared dinner and set the table the least they could do is put their dishes in the sink.

- She is so rude to my friends.

- If she would only tell me what she is thinking and how she feels.

- They forget that we were young once too.

- They have such expensive tastes, but they hate to work for anything.

- They want things that it has taken me twenty years to get.

- They are so talented. They can do anything they put their mind to.

- You would think that they could fix themselves a sandwich when I'm not there.

- All they do is fight—it drives me crazy.

- She thinks everything that is mine is also hers.

- I don't mind his using my tools, but why doesn't he put them back where he got them?

THE OTHER GUY'S OPINION

- He wants to take the car, but he never puts gas in it or volunteers to wash it.

- Every time he peels out of the driveway it scares me to death.

- He says I treat him like a child, but he doesn't act like an adult.

- She wants to live her own life, but the first time she runs into trouble she wants me to work it out.

- They are so irresponsible sometimes.

- When they really want to do something nothing stops them.

- I just don't understand how they think.

- Why would he want to skip school?

- He wanted the dog, but I have to take care of it.

- If she doesn't get off the phone, I'm going to think it is attached there permanently.

What Students Are Saying about Their Teachers

- He is really neat—he makes everything seem real.

- She really doesn't like me, so I know I'll get a lousy grade.

- He doesn't explain it so that I can understand it.

- He never has anything prepared—he just rambles on.

- I can't wait for her class. She's always teaching me things that are relevant in my life.

- Why can't they teach you something that you can use? I have taken history every year for eight years.

- Why does the coach always teach math? I understand it better than he does.

- She always plays favorites.

- He talks in a monotone; it puts me right to sleep. I wish he would talk less and we would do more things.

- She just gives us busy work all the time.

- There is no way I can get all this homework done. Don't they realize that I have other things to do?

- I love to go to her class. She lets you talk about things that interest you.

- He expects us to be as good an artist as he is and we are just learning.

- He stretches a 15-minute class into two hours.

- I could read the text and take a test in one week and learn more than I could learn a whole semester in his class.

- I swear I have taken this course three times. They just call it something different—that way I have to pay for it each time.

- Coaches just want to be athletes for the rest of their lives.

- He is always so grouchy.

- My teacher has bad breath.

- Her mind is always on something else.

- Her class is a piece of cake; she doesn't make you learn anything.

• He always has chalk all over his suit. I wonder if he ever gets it cleaned.

• She makes it seem so real that I feel like I'm really there.

• He gets so excited about science that I can't help but get excited too.

• He is such a push-over that all the guys are always bullying him. I don't know why he doesn't make them shape up.

• He thinks I'm really smart, and I can't let him down! So I study harder than I normally would.

• His classes are really hard, but you sure learn a lot.

• She's never really interested in your problems.

• He always takes time to explain things so you can understand them.

• She really listens to you when you talk to her.

• If she wears that dress one more day! Can't she afford to buy anything else?

What Teachers Are Saying about Their Students

• Give them an inch and they take a mile.

• If you keep them busy, they won't cause you any trouble.

• I could do a good job at teaching 10 or 15 students in a class but when it gets to be 30 or 40, forget it.

• You think nobody is listening and nobody cares and then you see someone catch the vision and it makes it all worthwhile.

• There should be less classroom lectures and more on-the-job training.

• It's hard to get kids excited about learning anymore because they are used to learning from TV—and who can compete with that?

• I love to teach, but I can't do it right with so many students because I don't have time to correct all those papers and tests.

• Kids don't learn any manners at home. I spend all my time teaching things their parents should have taught them.

• All kids want to do is sit in the lunchroom with their friends and goof off.

• Some kids are so irresponsible. You depend on them to do their part and they don't. Kids are getting smarter each year. That means that if you don't inspire and motivate them, they can think up more mischief to get into.

• Kids have no respect for personal property.

• When students get to college they can't spell, write, or do math. I can't understand it.

• Teaching is the most important job in the world and parents won't fight to pay teachers enough money to live on.

• Students aren't my worst problem—parents are.

• It seems like I spend all my time trying to motivate the underachiever and don't have time to work with the really bright kids.

• Some classes are fun and everyone learns a lot and in other classes you just can't seem to get the kids interested and excited.

• Kids will do anything to get your goat.

- I always direct my teaching to the kids who look interested and like to participate in class.

- Some days when I go to school I really fear for my life.

- We need to prepare students better for coping with today's world.

- Kids need to learn respect, courtesy, honesty, industriousness, how to get along with people, how to handle their money, how to be parents, how to buy a car, how to get a job, how to get a loan.

If we really listen, we can hear people reveal their innermost feelings—and that is definitely worth listening to.

Exterior Motivation   *Interior Motivation*

Some people have to be motivated by outside forces. Others can be motivated from within.

Compel or Impel?

Motivation is always more effective if the leader or parent tries to impel instead of compel. Compulsion is never a good method. It's much better to entice or persuade. A request invariably goes further than a demand.

A textile mill was having great difficulties with production. The workers were paid on a piece rate—but they just wouldn't produce. Their boss tried threats and force, but production didn't improve.

An expert was called in. He divided the workers into two groups. The first group was told that if they didn't get on the stick, they would lose their jobs. The second group was told that there was a problem—and that they were to help find a good solution.

The result? The production of the first group dropped lower and lower. As the pressure to produce went up, some workers quit, others rebelled. But morale in the second group quickly rose to an all-time high. Workers were given total responsibility for raising production—they could do whatever they wanted. They began to work together and come up with creative answers. In the first month alone, their productivity rose by 20 percent—all because they were impelled rather than compelled.

Parents and teachers know the compulsion approach works just as poorly with kids as it does with workers. Try to force them into a pattern and they'll end up turning the other way.

"Johnny, if you don't have this room cleaned by suppertime, you won't get anything to eat." What does Johnny do? He mopes and messes around, until finally supper comes and the room isn't clean. Then what does mother do? She either goes and helps him clean the room, or she relents: "Well, I'll let you eat, but you had better clean your room before you go to bed."

Either way, compulsion isn't the answer. Only persuasion works.

Attitude

Bruce Barton, a founding partner of the advertising firm of Batten, Barton, Durstine, and Osborne, shows how powerful a motivator attitude can be:

"One day on my first job as a young man in New York, a matter came up about which I happened to have the facts. My boss disagreed, and though I put up a good argument, he somewhat abruptly overruled me.

"I was living those days in a room in the 23rd Street Y.M.C.A. for which I paid seven dollars a week. His home was a fair-sized mansion requiring ten servants. The morning after our argument, the telephone rang while I was dressing, and I wondered who in New York could be after me so early.

"To my amazement it was the boss. Said he: 'I have been thinking about our discussion of yesterday, and I just want you to know that you were right and I was wrong.'

*"The boss with an income of $100,000 a year calls a $40-a-week youngster to say, 'I was wrong!' He had been one hundred percent with me; **after that he was the biggest man in town.***

"Years have gone by and I have known all sorts and conditions of men in business, the professions, and politics. As an employer of men and women in a modest way, it has interested me to observe how they divide into two classes: those who feel they have lowered themselves by admitting a mistake, and so try in every way to rationalize it, and those who come out in forthright fashion and admit the facts."

Reflecting

You've got all kinds of people in your organization. It's hard to deal with them all—and it seems that everyone needs a different kind of treatment.

But everyone also has an important thing in common: we all behave in a way that fits with the image we have of ourselves. We all make choices, and act on those choices, in ways that match our self-images.

If you can relate to people in a way that matches their image of themselves, you'll have a lot more success in motivating them. You'll be dealing not with the person you think you see, but the person they think you see.

It's a critical difference. You'll be able to communicate on a level they can understand.

220 Pound Weakling

For example, I once knew a man who felt inferior. He was tall and handsome; he stood six feet three inches and weighed in at

Reflect back to the other guy what he wants to see—that's communication on a level he can understand.

220. He was incredibly bright. But when I tried to deal with him as I saw him, I was totally unsuccessful. Because I was dealing with a person my friend didn't think existed.

So then I tried to see how he viewed himself. He dressed in sloppy clothes. He walked in hesitating steps. He let himself get discouraged easily by outside pressures. He drove an old, cruddy car.

In other words, he saw himself as a weakling who didn't have a lot of value in the world. Accordingly, he acted like a weakling. In fact, with his self-image, **he couldn't do otherwise.**

People get extremely frustrated when others try to treat them in ways that don't match their self-image. It doesn't matter whether that image is right or wrong—it's the only one they have. A weakling is disturbed if you treat him like he's strong, even if you think he's strong. An ugly person is offended if you treat him like he's handsome or beautiful, even if you see nothing ugly about him.

Becoming What You Imagine

Self-image always precedes the choices people make. Those choices are reflected in the person's dress, actions, environment, language, and so forth. Communicate with that image and you have a powerful tool for motivating the person.

Reflecting Back What They Want to See

Dealing with the other person's image of himself, not your image of him, is called reflecting. The process takes three steps:

• **Assess.** Determine what is the person's self-image. How does he see himself? How does he dress, what is his job, how does he walk, what kind of car does he drive, what is his favorite word, what are his mannerisms, how does he deal with his working and living environment, what are his hobbies,what kind of friends does he choose, what does he do for recreation? Stay objective and assess the answers to those questions. Forget your image of the person and learn about his.

• **Reflect.** When you talk with that person or deal with him in any way, deal with his self-image. Meet him on his own level. Match your actions and reactions to the image he's projecting.

• **Appeal.** Use that image to convey the things you want him to do. In your appeal, mirror (reflect) his use of language and mannerisms and actions. Using this process, you'll be able to motivate him to do the things that need to be done. At the same time, you can build him as a person by helping him to develop a more positive self-image. **But only if you reflect the image he's starting with.**

I once had an experience that shows how powerful the self-image really is. I have a friend who couldn't carry a tune if a gun were held to his back. One day we went together to a hypnotist's show, and my friend soon found himself up on stage singing.

I was amazed. I've heard my friend sing before, and his voice is awful. It's the kind that makes you wish you had brought cotton for your ears. But that night, at the hypnotist's suggestion, my friend sang with a clear and beautiful voice!

What made the difference? For a while, the hypnotist changed my friend's self-image, and suddenly he had new "powers."

Unfortunately, though, the change wasn't permanent. We can't walk around being hypnotized all the time. Neither can our workers. So until our workers change their self-images, making them the ideal and perfect people we wish they'd be, there is only one solution. Deal with them on the level they're at now. Approach them on the level of their present image. Only with that approach will the sequence of assess, reflect, and appeal work for us.

Push or Pull?

The organization you belong to has a great influence on you and on all your people. It has its own personality. And, like it or not, that personality has a great deal to do with how everyone functions in the company or department.

An Organization's Personality

There are basically two kinds of organizational personalities:

The first pushes. It pushes people down, pushes them back, holds them, prevents their growth.

The second pulls. It pulls people up, pulls them forward, lifts them, helps them develop and grow.

It's hard for a person not to be affected by the personality his organization has. Some people will succeed no matter what; and some will fail. But most are afflicted (or blessed) by their organization's personality.

It's difficult to grow when someone else is constantly pushing you down.

Descriptive Words

You can tell which kind of organization you work for by the adjectives you use to describe it. It usually only takes one or two:

exciting	drudgery	commonplace
mechanical	paranoid	intellectual
unified	arrogant	diligent
immature	erratic	envious
deaf	prompt	chaotic
sincere	pompous	overbearing

Take a good look at the list and pick out the adjectives that you think best describe your organization. Those descriptive words will give you an important piece of information: is your organization a pusher or a puller?

The personality of any organization determines the quality of work it does. It also determines how effective the efforts at motivation will be.

Providing a Climate for Growth

Which kind of organization do you belong to—a pusher or a puller?

All around us we see organizations that are described as uptight, critical, pressured. How can its managers create an open, innovative atmosphere? They can't!
If an organization is described as distrustful, how can its managers create an atmosphere of loyalty? They can't!

On the other hand, if an organization is described as exciting, how can its managers create a static atmosphere? It's hard—they have to consciously try!

The level of performance of the people in an organization can often be directly linked to that organization's personality. If you think your people need motivation, look first at your organization. Is it a pusher or a puller? If you see a pusher, you'll need to make some changes in the organization itself before you can do the things you want with your people.

Kind of Organization

We've looked at what we can learn from descriptive adjectives. They will tell you how you feel about your organization. But how do others feel—your co-workers, your superiors, your subordinates? The answer lies in what they say. Which of the following do workers say about your company?

Pushing	Pulling
"The company holds people down."	"The company lifts people up."
"The old way is good enough."	"That sounds like a great new idea."
"If you want to buy that, you need to go through channels."	"We're given freedom over our own budgets."
"Sorry, but eight-to-five is a requirement of this job."	"Schedules are flexible as long as we get the job done,"
"No, you cannot take a late lunch."	"Late lunch? Sure. Things here are fine."
"I don't see it in the manual so I guess we can't do it."	"It's not in the manual, but it's okay to try it anyway."
"We're not hired to think."	"Maybe this approach would work."
"The important thing here is to be able to follow orders."	"Management is considering this change. From your perspective, do you think it would work?"

Do you work for a pusher or a puller? Pushers have a hard time motivating their people—the workers constantly feel like they're not important, like they're an insignificant cog in an uncaring wheel. Pullers are effective motivators—they help their workers feel that each person counts, and that each person is able to make an important contribution to the company.

Remember this: it's impossible to advance by pushing back—only by pulling ahead!

Riding a Dead Horse

Here's what was overheard from the board room of the Acme Buggywhip Company during its final hours. The boss is speaking:

"Now, I know people are saying these new auto-mobiles are all the rage. I'll tell you, you'd have to be an idiot to want to ride one of those godforsaken contraptions. They make noise and scare the horses off the road and belch out smoke and make a mess. Don't worry about them. They're just a passing fad. They'll never really catch on.

"Oh, people might try them for a day or two, but that will be it. Then they'll see that autos are un-American and uncivilized. Anyone who cares about baseball, mother, and apple pie will stick with the horse and buggy. And we know that makes up 98 percent of the buying public!

"So, men, listen to me. We'll just keep on and let these cars die their own quick death. We'll keep on and make our company bigger and better. It will be at the forefront of a new generation of buggywhips!

Dead horses don't get very far, and neither do the people who ride them.

"In fact, to show you my faith in our future, I've just authorized the building of a brand-new plant!"

Ego Investments

Sometimes people get so involved in their pet projects that they can't see the forest for the trees. They can't see that they're driving at ninety miles an hour in reverse.

69

And the sad part of it is that usually those people end up taking others with them. Too often managers have their best people working on the worst possible projects.

Peter Drucker calls those kinds of projects "investments in managerial ego." Such projects most often focus on the past and are usually just past their prime.

Which is exactly where the good worker should not be. He will be most useful working on tomorrow's projects—not yesterday's.

Effective motivation puts the best people on the best projects—the ones that will produce the best possible future results. Only by letting people give their best to a project that has a future will a manager get their best. If he puts them on jobs that chase the past, his whole organization will end up in yesterday.

Here's what was overheard from the board room of the Acme Car Company in Detroit during their final hours. The boss is speaking:

"Now, I know that people are saying these new foreign cars are all the rage. I'll tell you, you'd have to be an idiot to want to ride in one of those godforsaken contraptions. They're cramped and small and don't give a comfortable ride and have absolutely no power. Don't worry about them. They're just a passing fad. They'll never really catch on.

"So, men, listen to me. We'll just keep on and let these foreign cars die their own quick death. We'll just ignore them, and you'll see how quickly they go away!

"In fact, to show you my faith in our future, I've just authorized a brand-new plant to be built!"

Getting Inside Without Surgery

What motivates people? I'm talking far below the surface, deep down inside—what really motivates?

The question is a difficult one to answer. Cutting someone open to see what's inside doesn't help. And, sometimes asking doesn't work either! Many people don't know what really motivates them, or if they do know, they probably have a hard time expressing it.

The only accurate way to find out what motivates a person is by objective observation. You can learn the dominant needs and concerns of another person by looking at the choices he makes.

Choice Indicators

People behave consistently with how they see themselves. They form a self-image early in life, and all of their choices are made consistent with that image. If you read all the choices a person makes, you will see that those choices form a consistent pattern. This pattern can illuminate their dominant needs and concerns—and those

To find out what really motivates a person, you have to learn how to look inside his head.

elements will prove to be motivating factors in his life.

People make choices about how they walk, talk, and the mannerisms they use. They make choices about toothpaste, clothing, cleanliness, and hairstyle. They make choices about their homes, cars, jobs. About gestures. About posture.

If you can read the choices a person makes, you'll know how to read the individual. You'll start to gather data about him. And pretty soon that data will fall into patterns. The patterns will tell you what motivates him.

What Makes a Person Tick?

I once knew a manager who suffered from low self-esteem. She constantly felt threatened by others. How did she show it? She had a hard time giving others credit. She tried to build up her own name in the department, while tearing others down. She made a successful attempt to move her office closer to the big boss's.

This manager was a true bureaucrat. She treated people like they were simply tools for her own accomplishment. If someone got out of line, they were promptly moved out of the department—or fired.

Those who worked with her didn't take the trouble to find out what made this woman tick. They jumped to conclusions and just thought she was cranky and kingdom-building. But if they had taken the trouble to do a little observing, they would have seen the sure signs of low self-esteem.

Parents and teachers who are concerned with motivating kids can learn a lot about what's inside them by watching their choices.

For example, a kid may make these kinds of choices:

• grows his hair long and scraggly
• wears messy clothes
• doesn't want to do his homework
• gets addicted to video games
• hangs around with other kids just like him

Those choices tell a lot about that person. He cares a great deal about his peers, and he'll do just about anything to gain their approval.

Get inside the other person and you'll know how to motivate him. In this case, motivate the teenager through his peers. Use the things they expect of him to help you get him to do what you want.

Here's another example. An employee in a major company suffered from insecurity. (You'll find them all over.) Change was threatening to him. His manager thought the employee was simply in a rut, that he didn't like new approaches purely because he was lazy or being obstinate. He tried to motivate the employee with threats—but that only made the problem worse, because then the employee felt more insecure than ever.

But then the manager began reading the choices the employee made: he wore the same clothes all the time, followed the same daily routine, told the same old jokes over and over, resisted any change in work procedure, lived in the same home forever, had the same friends, and so on. The manager started to see the emerging pattern. It showed him that the employee could best be motivated by bolstering his security.

Objective Answer

When we watch the choices people make, we see what matters most to them, and then we can motivate them accordingly. Once we know what makes them tick, we'll know how to wind their stems! Here's an example of how effective this can be:

"An old frame church in New England stood in desperate need of exterior paint, so the minister recruited a half-dozen volunteers from his congregation. But he couldn't get them to show up for the job—until he had a devilish inspiration. He divided the building into six segments, then, in bold letters three feet high, painted a volunteer's name on each segment. Shortly thereafter, each recruit dutifully arrived to paint his segment, fulfill his pledge—and avoid all that public notoriety."
    Dudley Lynch, *Kiwanis* Magazine, Oct. 76.

Energy Limit

Every minute of every day we're using up energy. But we don't have an unlimited amount to count on.

Each of us has a limited amount of energy to use each day. If we use a lot of energy in one activity, less remains for other tasks.

The amount available differs from one person to the next. And the amount used in a given task differs from one person to the next.

Draining and Charging Our Batteries

It's like we are each a large battery. Each battery has a limited amount of energy available to it—but the demands are almost unlimited. First you light up one 50-watt bulb. Then you need to light up a 100-watt bulb as well. Then a motor is attached to your battery. Each new problem adds another drain on your battery. So far you're all right. But if another energy drain is attached, you're in trouble.

An employee, like a battery, can give out only so much energy.

The newly divorced employee has a real energy drain from the breakup. Then he has a flat tire on the way to work. Another drain. He didn't get enough sleep last night. A drain. He has bill problems. A drain. Then his boss expects him to finish that report by Thursday.

Each new problem creates another drain on his available energy. If he's not careful he'll soon run out of power. He will be unable to move in any direction.

How does all this fit into motivation?

You can't keep draining a battery beyond its power supply, insisting that it give and give and give. It has only so much energy to give. If you take too much out of it, you only end up with a dead battery. Then you'll have a lot of downtime while you recharge it again. People need to be recharged. Time, encouragement, a change of scenery can all create more energy flowing in than out.

Each Person's Energy Level

Recognize your workers' energy levels. Don't expect more than they can give. That's unfair to everyone.

When a manager places unrealistic expectations on his people, their motivation goes down. When he recognizes that fluctuating energy levels are a fact of life, and places expectations accordingly, motivation and effectiveness go up.

I remember a conversation with an old guy. After two beers, as he was feeling loose and comfortable, he said, "My mother-in-law just left. I'm totally drained. It's like she puts a big straw into my head and sucks out all my energy." He took another swig of beer, casually wiped his mouth, and continued. "Now my brother, that's a different story. He fills me up, instead of taking away. I'm always sad to see him leave, he makes me feel so good!"

Tips for Motivators

When people feel good about them-selves, it's easier for them to be motivated. Why? Because when they have high self-esteem, they're not worried about how they relate to the world. They're not worried about what others are thinking about them. They've "got it all together." And their motivator will benefit from their self-confidence. Here are some ways to help your people feel better about themselves:

- In conversation, whether casual or formal, give your undivided attention. That will help them see they are important to you.

- When you give out a responsibility, let them do it their way. And don't take it back if you feel things aren't going well.

- Involve workers in resolving conflicts with co-workers.

- Learn to express your feelings honestly, and let your workers do the same.

- Admit when you make a mistake.

- Let each worker express himself creatively within the parameters allowed by his job.

- Look for the good in what the person is doing, not just the bad.

- Avoid put-downs.

- Show your workers that you trust them.

- Avoid comparisons between one worker and another.

- Be fair.

- Separate the worker from his acts. When there's a problem, let the worker know that you're displeased with what he did, not with him as a person.

- Share the power of decision making.

- Don't require more of the worker than he is able to do. (If he can't measure up to the needed standards, it will be doing everyone a favor to help him work else-where.)

- Avoid favoritism.

- Be kind and considerate. Set clear rules—and be consistent in enforcing them.

Exhortation is the most commonly used motivational technique. It is also the least effective.

"You Really Ought to Be a Better Manager, You Know!"

Exhortation is the most common motivational approach in the world. It's also the least effective.

Just insisting someone ought to do something does absolutely no good. Take this self-quiz and you'll see what I mean: read the exhortation at the top of this page. Does it motivate you to go out and do better? I'll be on pretty safe ground if I say it probably doesn't. It may have even had the opposite effect, making you feel defensive or justified about your present performance.

Exhortations All over the Place

- **Parent to child:** "You really ought to keep your room clean, you know."

- **Politician to voter:** "You really ought to be more actively involved in the issues of your community, you know."

- **Kid to dog:** "You really shouldn't poop on our front lawn, you know."

- **Teacher to student:** "You really ought to study harder, you know."

- **Boss to worker:** "You really ought to be more productive, you know.

Keep Working with Something That Never Works

And how much real good do these exhortations do? Not much. More than likely, they make things even worse than they were before.

In his *Language in Thought and Action*, S.I. Hayakawa wrote:

"In order to cure (what she believes to be) her husband's faults, a wife may nag him. His faults get worse, so she nags him some more. Naturally his faults get worse still, and she nags him even more. Governed by a fixated reaction to the problem of her husband's faults, she can meet it only one way. The longer she continues, the worse it gets, until they are both nervous wrecks; their marriage is destroyed, and their lives are shattered."

What I'm saying is you really shouldn't try to exhort your people into better performance, you know.

The Ten Commandments of Motivational Failure

Here are ten things to do if you would like to create a totally unmotivated, unproductive company. (Maybe you have already tried one or two!)

1 Thou shalt reward the boss and his cronies for successes brought about by their subordinates in the company.

2 Thou shalt try to be all things to all people at all times.

3 Thou shalt stress activity over results. Thou shalt assume that how thy workers do their job is more important than why they are doing it.

4 Thou shalt discourage creative thinking by all but the top level of management. Make it publicly known that only the highest paid have good ideas.

5 Thou shalt try something else when everything is going well.

6 Thou shalt keep very tight control over such decisions as buying paper clips and making copies on the copy machine and who parks where. And thou shalt seek no control over what the company's business is and how to best utilize your people's potential.

7 Thou shalt create a complex organizational structure, loaded down with all imaginable levels of bureaucracy.

8 Thou shalt have little or no contact with thy customers—they only complicate business anyway.

9 Thou shalt emphasize productivity through programs and systems and things rather than through people.

10 Thou shalt keep a lot of people on thy staff—bigger is always better.

Responsibility

An intersection on a small country road in Indiana was serviced by a four-way stop. The four-way stop worked well for years, but as the area grew more and more, people began to complain about the congestion at the stop. "Can't we have a traffic light?" they asked the county officials.

Finally a traffic light was installed. As traffic in the growing community increased, so did the accident rate. In fact, the accident rate increased at a much higher rate than did the traffic.

It was very confusing. People thought the light would make the intersection safer. What could be the problem? Why were there so many more accidents?

It's the Light's Responsibility

I don't know if they ever resolved the issue, but I know what the source of their problem was. It lies in responsibility. At the four-way stop, each driver felt personally responsible for his own welfare. Since everyone had to stop and wait his turn before he could proceed (and even then he had to be cau-

tious), a driver knew it was his own darn fault if he got in an accident.

But at the stoplight it was a whole different story. The responsibility for traffic control shifted from the drivers to the light. It was no longer the drivers' responsibility to look out for other people; it was simply the light's responsibility to stop them.

That stoplight problem gives us an important principle in management: **The development of responsibility is inseparably linked to the amount of control a person has.**

The more control a person feels over a situation, the more responsibility he will exhibit. The less control, the less responsibility.

Wanting Responsibility—Giving Control

If you want to motivate others to be more responsible, give them more control. We've all worked for this guy: "Why can't people take more responsibility around here?" he grumps. "If I want anything done right I have to do it myself!"

He's not kidding either. His problem is that he may verbally give responsibilities, but he won't pass on control at the same time. The control he clutches tightly to himself. He indicates who does what and when and how. He dictates the way things need to be done.

He does it all. He believes the problem lies in workers who won't take responsibility. "I've got the biggest motivational problem the world has ever seen," he moans. "Just take a look at those people who work for me!"

If only he'd give his people control along with the token responsibility. Then they'd really shine!

Fixing a Locked Car

To give responsibility without control is like the guy who took his car to the garage to be fixed. "There's an awful thump in the engine," he explained. "And I need the tires rotated. Put the spare on the left rear—it's in the trunk. I'll be back at 4 p.m. " Off he goes.

But before he leaves he takes care to lock the trunk and all the doors and take the keys with him.

He returns at 4 p.m. The work is not done. In fact, they haven't even moved his car! "I just knew it," he mutters to himself. "You can't trust anyone to take responsibility!"

Rules of the Game

Everyone carries around a set of basic beliefs through which he sees the world and himself. This list of beliefs is the person's connecting link with the world. Everything about how he acts (or reacts) is determined by his base beliefs.

When everyone working together shares similar beliefs, things really go well. But, too often, two people are trying to play the same game using different sets of rules. They think they're going after the same thing—but one is really playing Monopoly while the other is playing gin rummy.

The more employees share similar beliefs, the more similar their work will be. The more a company's workers share a belief in the importance of productivity, the more productive they will tend to be. The more people in any group share positive beliefs, the more effective they'll be.

Self-fulfilling Prophecy

It is as if each of us has a window hanging in front of our faces. On the window is written the beliefs that govern our actions. We cannot see the world without filtering it through those beliefs.

These beliefs determine what you do in life. They become a sort of self-fulfilling prophecy. One person's window says, "I can't do math." Because he doesn't believe in himself, he fails. And then he says, "See, I told you I couldn't do math."

A group will say, "We can work well only with each other." When an outsider comes in, the whole effort fails. Everything goes to pot. Then the group says, "See, we told you we could work well only with each other."

The kinds of beliefs that run our lives come in many forms. Here are a few I've heard from people I know:

"I can't make more than $24,000 a year."

"People should always do their best."

"Work is the cost of pleasure."

"If I don't take advantage of it, someone else will."

? *What is written on your belief window about:*

Confidence	Energy
Attitude	"Do it now!"
Diligence	Decisiveness
Resilience	Discipline
Self-Reliance	Conviction
Enthusiasm	Punctuality
Authority	Persistence
Creativity	Productivity
Empathy	Patience
Ability to Change	Good Judgment
Outgoingness	Aggressiveness
Concentration	Ability to Relax
Positive Attitude	Submissiveness

Think how much our lives are controlled by these beliefs:

"Kids are irresponsible. They won't do anything you ask them."

"People in organizations are like sheep: they look to their leader for guidance before they'll do a single thing."

A Belief in Productivity

Reasons for Japanese productivity have been sought for more than two decades. What is the answer? Is it the programs or techniques or approaches?

Actually, it's none of the above.

Processes or methods are not the answer. I believe the answer lies in the shared beliefs of the Japanese workers.

Consider the difference between Japanese and Western productivity. There's an incredible gap between the two. And virtually all the difference lies in the shared beliefs of

the Japanese workers! Their beliefs become a self-fulfilling prophecy that leads to the kind of results every manager dreams about.

Somehow we Americans insist on doing everything backwards. We want to increase profits, so we keep working on methods to increase productivity. The solution doesn't lie in the methods. It lies in positive beliefs, commonly shared. If we would simply help our people change their negative and divisive beliefs, then the increased productivity would be a natural result.

Other Beliefs

Shared beliefs can make a difference in other ways. Suppose you're a teacher in a classroom and the students share this belief:

"We're not as good as the kids in the private school down the road."

How will your kids act? Unfortunately, they'll fulfill their own prophecy, and they won't do nearly as well as the kids in the school down the road.

But what if you as the teacher can change those beliefs? What if you can get them to believe this:

"We're every bit as good as the kids in the private school."

Then they'll start to act like it.

And what if you can take it a step further and they start to believe this:

"We're a heck of a lot better than the kids in any other school in town, including the private schools."

Then they fulfill that prophecy and become the best students around.

The same thing can happen in a club, a service organization, a youth group, a church group, a family. "We're the best. We have the ability to do what's needed, when it's needed. United we stand—and we stand stronger than anyone else around."

Our beliefs become the rules of our own games. If we think we're great, we'll have the ability to play a good game of life, and win at every step. But if we, and the group we're with, think we're not too hot, we'll subconsciously make it come to pass.

Want to motivate? Get to the other person through his positive beliefs. Then he won't have any choice but to perform at his very best.

Compare Japanese beliefs to American beliefs:

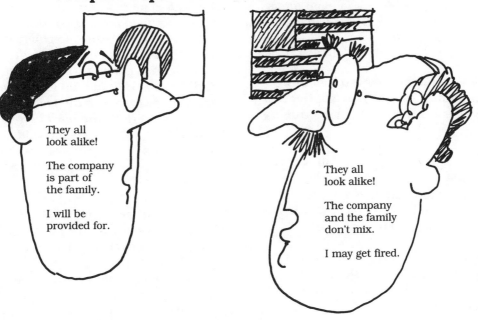

They all
look alike!

The company
is part of
the family.

I will be
provided for.

They all
look alike!

The company
and the family
don't mix.

I may get fired.

Kick Starting

Changing human behavior without understanding motivation is like trying to start a stalled car by kicking it.

Ernest Dichter

The more a manager understands how people (including himself) are motivated, the more success he'll have at producing results.

With some people, it seems that all they know of human nature is that if you kick them they will move! Such people lack the real starter: an understanding of why people act as they do—and what to do about it.

In *Psychology Today*, Margie Casady tells of how an old man motivated others to do what he wanted—just by being aware of human behavior:

The old man was bothered by the boys' noisy play—but he didn't yell at them. Instead he offered them each a quarter if they would play noisily closer to his house. The youngsters raced back the following day and made a tremendous racket in front of the house. The old man paid them, and asked them to return the next day.

Again they made noise, and again the old man paid them for it. But this time he gave each boy only 20 cents, explaining that he was running out of money. On the following day, they got only 15 cents each. Furthermore, the old man told them, he would have to reduce the fee to five cents on the fourth day. The boys became angry, and told the old man they would not be back. It was not worth the effort, they said, to make noise for only five cents a day.

Understanding the behavior of others is as easy as watching what they do and then coming to correct conclusions about why they're doing it. The keys are, first, observing—and then correctly figuring out what need the person was fulfilling; second, doing this observation objectively without personal needs and wants fogging up the view.

"We understand behavior when we know what caused it or what made the person do it."

Norman Maier

And when we understand behavior, we have in our hands the secrets of effective motivation.

Alignment

In the 1920s the Hawthorne Plant of Western Electric Company found itself with a big productivity problem on its hands. No one could really define what the problem was—it seemed that the workers were getting everything they might want.

So management decided to try a series of experiments to see if they could get the people motivated. They divided the plant into two groups: the control group, who continued as usual, and the test group.

In the first experiment, they increased the light in the room where the test group worked. Productivity went up! They put light back at normal levels and the productivity dropped back to where it was. Just to make sure of their findings, they dropped the light below normal—and were very surprised to see that productivity rose again.

It was most confusing. At first they had thought they had the answer: more light. But now they weren't sure. So they tried some other tactics:

They required the test group to do a certain amount of work per day rather than have them put in a set number of hours. Productivity rose.

They gave them two five-minute rest periods. Productivity rose.

They gave them a fifteen-minute break with a hot snack. Productivity rose.

They let everyone go home an hour early. Productivity rose.

They had everyone stay at work an extra hour. Productivity rose.

Then they stopped experimenting and put everything back to normal. Productivity rose to an all-time high!

The Final Conclusion

In the end, the researchers could reach only one reasonable conclusion: the experiment had made the test group feel important. And that alone had been sufficient to cause productivity to climb.

Give Them X When They Want Y

Too often managers assume they know what their employees want and proceed to give it to them. They'll raise the light level, or lower it—when all along the employees want something else. When the expected results don't come, the manager wonders what went wrong. He or she looks for elaborate answers—when the real answer is simply this: the things the employee got didn't line up with what he needed.

Just after you open up great new opportunities, your best people resign.

You've put all your people through an expensive in-house educational program, but performance remains the same.

The workers band together in a union right after your best offer ever.

That high-paid consultant gave you exactly what you wanted, but it doesn't seem to make any difference.

Those new programs work for a while, but then it's right back to where you were before.

You just gave your daughter some new freedoms—and now she's acting worse than ever.

The family said they wanted to have family councils to work out problems, but all they do there is go at each other's throats.

Your group enthusiastically voted to raise some money for a special trip. But you, as the leader, are the only one who's willing to do any work for it.

The answer to all those problems is the same: **The more the motivator is able to align what he gives his people with what they really want and need, the better the results will be.**
Reaching that ideal comes through three steps:

- The motivator needs to have a clear idea of what he wants.

- The motivator needs to have a clear idea of what his people want.

- If the two areas of want are in conflict, one or the other will have to change. Only when the wants align can the desired results be achieved.

Fertilizing Results

Recently my neighbor sent his kid out to fertilize the lawn. The kid's method was noteworthy: he scattered it about very quickly, getting some areas well and missing other spots completely.

Apparently my friend's family was conspiring in a special family program: "Let's develop patience in Dad!"

Where the fertilizer fell, the grass grew better. Where the fertilizer missed, it didn't grow so well. You can imagine how the lawn looked as a whole—just like a patchwork quilt.

Fertilizer works in our society just the way it does on our lawns. **What the organizational system rewards the most is what you get the most of.**

What You Get Is What You Reward

Suppose you reward your workers or children or prospects for indifference—you get more indifference.

Suppose you reward for purposeful activity—that's what you'll get more of.

In a garden, what is fertilized and cared for grows the best and produces the most. Should growing people be any different?

Suppose you reward for surface professionalism only—guess what you'll get.

Here's a key of motivation: determine what end result you want, and reward only for those things that will lead to it. If you want production, reward for production. And certainly don't reward for laziness or nonproduction.

You can see how fertilizer works in all professions. It will work in yours too.

The Medical Profession

Doctors are rewarded only when people are sick. The longer the patient's recuperation, the more the doctor's reward. In other words, the fertilizer is applied freely to induce the doctor to find out you really are sick—and keep you that way. Does it work? A congressional committee recently estimated that Americans had spent $4 billion on unnecessary operations that year.

The Chinese apply the fertilizer differently: they pay a doctor to keep them well. If they get sick, the doctor stops getting paid. You can bet that those doctors are experts in preventive medicine.

The Legal Profession

Lawyers are rewarded only when their clients are in trouble. How do they keep them in trouble? Increased contention, interpretation and reinterpretation, proliferation of legalese. The longer the case drags out, the more money they get. So they ask for extensions, recesses, and the like. Our society is being crushed under the weight of its own legal system. Why? Because of the effective way we've fertilized.

The Teaching Profession

Teachers get fertilized too: the more students they can control, the more paperwork they can go through, the longer they serve—all these add up to more reward. Their main activity ends up as being high-paid baby-sitters. Not because that's their first preference, but because that's where the fertilizer is being applied.

A proposal was recently made to base the educational system on the gains made by the students. The teacher would be paid according to how effective he was. But the teachers' union would have none of that. They knew which side of their bread their manure was spread on.

Some systems are working better. In private schools teachers are often fertilized for student performance. And, of course, their students do much better.

And a Cop

Some policemen are paid more when they are able to give out more tickets. The policeman in Jordan Valley, Oregon, is paid a percentage of all the fines he gives out. The town has a very small population, but they do have a good budget. Especially from all the out-of-towners who pass through and pay fines. One year the policeman there made $102,000.

It's all a matter of how and where you spread it.

You can apply this principle in your motivation. If you want someone to do better, simply fertilize him better. Give rewards for what you want to get. If your employee or student is giving you weeds, don't make them grow bigger by rewarding him for it. Give him the reward only when he gives you good grass—and the grass will get better and better.

Competition

I was raised on a farm, and my father swore by the two-cow theory.

Here's how the two-cow theory works. If you get one cow, he'll graze your pasture and eventually get fat enough to take to market. You'll make good money off of him. But if you get two cows, suddenly they each have competition for the good grazing areas. That competition—plus having some company—makes both cows grow faster and stronger. The sum of the two together is greater than the sum of the two raised separately. The competition increases production.

Competition—The Two-Cow Theory

Businesses aren't exempt from the two-cow theory. If a business doesn't have any competition, it has no one to set the pace besides itself. The result is most often severe motivational problems. What applies to a business as a whole, of course, also applies to individual workers in that business.

The same thing happens in a classroom. I remember that the only thing that got me through high school with halfway-decent grades was the two-cow theory. Another student and I had similar interests and skills—and soon found ourselves in a friendly competition. After each test or paper or presentation we'd get together and compare our scores. It got to be a real contest. And, without ever intending it, we soon found our grades rapidly climbing. All because of the thrill of competition.

Consider a runner on a fast track. Running alone, he will never set any records. Neither will his biggest rival. But put the two of them side by side on that track. Suddenly both of them are running faster. And both of them might set a new record.

Without competition, your organization and its individual employees cannot develop to their full potential.

Without competition—

- the only standard is self-imposed;
- there is no reason to reach higher;
- there is no fear of failure or of being beaten out of business by someone else.

All of that is destructive. A lot of business-men curse their competition, but they're mistaken. It is competition that makes their business as strong as it is. The two-cow theory.

The Problem of No Competition

If your business lacks competition, look out. Your ideas may be too new. You may bear the sole cost of breaking in the idea with the public. It could even be that your kind of business holds no value to the public.

And without competition, you're going to have some serious motivation problems.

If your employees aren't competitive, watch out. Competition motivates. It causes everyone to do better.

If your students aren't competitive in the classroom, start looking for lower grades. Some students aren't motivated by the grades themselves, but only by the excitement of trying to outdo someone else.

If the players on the football field aren't competitive, resign yourself to a losing season. The competition would motivate them to do better and better each time. But the lack of it makes them complacent and apathetic.

The Soviets have a noncompetitive, closed work system. It's a stagnant system. Their five-year plans show that they expect less production in that time, not more.

The Soviet system is dying. The country's soul is dying. The workers' motivation is dead.

All because there is no place for competition in the system. All living systems need competition. It's an element of survival.

We Need Competition

• Athens needed Sparta.
• Caesar needed the Gauls.
• AT&T needs MCI.

Your company needs its competitor.

Your employees need to have competition in the ranks.

Your students need to compete with each other. When they don't, they stop excelling.

Children in a family need healthy competition. It's the only way they'll ever grow.

Give your people something to compete for. It won't demoralize the losers—especially if there's more than one prize. It will only make all of them do better than ever before.

Did you ever see a good horse-race with only one horse?

Different Strokes for Different Folks

It's surprising, but most managers don't really know what their employees want. A study was recently done to see what employees want most—and to see what the bosses thought their people wanted most. Compare these two priority listings (1 is considered most important; 10 is least):

What Managers Think Employees Want		What Employees Really Want
1	Good pay	5
2	Job security	4
3	Promotion and growth	6
4	Good working conditions	7
5	Interesting work	1
6	Tactful discipline	10
7	Loyalty to employees	8
8	Full appreciation of work done	2
9	Help with personal problems	9
10	Feeling of being in on things	3

Study by Kenneth Kovoch, reported in the *Advanced Management Journal.*

The failure to perceive what people really need is the biggest motivational problem there is.

Managers must constantly remember that employees rarely, if ever, perceive things the way a manager does. Just because a person does the same actions as yourself doesn't mean that he's motivated by the same needs. He may have an entirely different way of expressing himself.

The only way to accurately tell what motivates a person is by objectively observing him—and listening to him.

Common Needs—Unique Wants

Human needs are common to all people—security, food, self-esteem, and so forth. But wants are unique expressions of individuality. Wants are perceptually based on beliefs of how things should be.

Assumed Needs

We project onto others what we think and what we have experienced. But their reasons, needs, wants, and motivations may be entirely different. For example, when you see people eating you may assume that they are hungry. Why? Because that's what your personal experience indicates to you. Yet they may not be hungry at all. Instead they might be eating to be part of the group. Or they may be eating because going to that particular restaurant raises their self-esteem.

Oftentimes we don't even understand ourselves that well. We think we know what we want, but we fail to see the need that drives our wants. For example:

A manager thinks:	But the truth is:
He wants to be boss.	He needs security.
He wants an expensive car.	He needs self-esteem.
She wants to be famous.	She needs more love.
He wants to be rich.	He needs fulfillment.
She wants a part-time job.	She needs freedom.

Effective motivation is based on reality.
The more you find out a person's real needs, the more effective your motivation efforts will be. Only when the manager knows a person's true motivation will he be able to meet that person's needs. And only when he meets the needs will he be able to be the motivating force for that person.

A New Kind of Worker

Nowadays we have a new kind of worker doing a new kind of work. In the past few decades, people's attitudes toward work have undergone a drastic change. Failing to recognize this change is an invitation to fail.

Managers need to recognize this: **Old methods and expectations of performance will increasingly fail in future job settings.**

The seventeenth-century management mentality just doesn't work with a twentieth-century employee. The manager who tries antiquated methods will invariably end up frustrated.

A New Approach

What is needed for today is a new approach, a basic change in management concepts. Approaches to motivation must be considered carefully. Too often a manager tries to motivate his or her people as though they were brainless serfs or slaves. That may have worked with serfs and slaves, but it won't work with the employee of the twentieth century.

Look at how different the world has become:

Multiple choices

It used to be that if a person didn't like working for his overlord he was just out of luck. There was nowhere else to go. (How many castles were there to clean, after all?) But that isn't the case anymore. A worker usually has a broad range of choices. If things aren't to his liking in one company, he can move to another.

More control

The worker today doesn't just do what he's told. No one's starving to death anymore, at least in the industrialized nations. People have more control over their destiny. Oftentimes they have almost total control over their work, too. The manager doesn't know how to do their jobs; he just knows (hopefully) how to manage. If the job is going to be done right, it will have to be done by the workers. This gives them a great deal of control on the job—and increasingly, employees are demanding a right to participate in decisions that affect their jobs.

Change

Things are changing faster and faster, both in technology and in individual mentality. As the world around us changes, workers change with it. What is the norm today will be outdated tomorrow.

From Back to Head

The great majority of work in days past was done with the body. Hard physical labor was the norm, and most people had to work just to survive. That's no longer the case. The work of ages past—generation, production, and storage of goods—has shifted to a new emphasis. The mind has replaced the body as the primary tool.

> *"Primitive man was driven—by cold and hunger and thirst—to perform certain acts. Modern technological man is led—through the manipulation of symbols—to choose the directions in which he will expend his energy."*
>
> Don Faban

Trying to use old motivational methods with today's employees is like trying to get a car to go faster by using a buggy whip. The whip may have worked on the horse, but with a car you just end up scratching the paint.

What Works Today?

Benefits are nice—but dangling the carrot isn't all it's cracked up to be. The critical thing is your employees' perceptions. We know that people act the way they do because of how they perceive the world.

When a manager wants to motivate his people, he shouldn't try to change their world. He shouldn't try to change outside conditions. He should work with the inner man. Once he changes how his employees think and feel inside, he'll have been successful in changing how they act. For the better.

> *"There seems to be some evidence that a new type of man is appearing."*
>
> Pierre Bertaux

In olden times, people were driven by basic needs to work—and they put up with all kinds of crap in the process . . .

. . . But now things are different. The manager who tries to drive his workers to increased production ends up with no workers.

Management Styles

Managers often come in two extreme styles, whether they're teachers, parents, salesmen, or businessmen. The first extreme is the total libertarian. He's a live-and-let-live guy, a guy who puts his feet up on his desk and says, "Aw, what the hell!"

The second type is the complete authoritarian. He's rigid and unbending. The authoritarian wants to have a say in when you breathe and how deeply. His attitude is: "You're going to get hell!" And if there's not a reason for getting you into trouble, he'll find one!

Both extremes often lead to failure. With the libertarian, the group collapses from inactivity. With the authoritarian, it freezes up with rigor mortis.

Failure by Nepotism

Not too many years ago a man inherited his father's business, a department store chain that had been in business for over 100 years. Things were booming. The future was bright and rosy for the heir. But in less than 10 years he was standing in bankruptcy court. The entire chain had fallen down around his ears.

What was the problem? His management style. He was the libertarian type. He spent his days in fun and games—and it was only a matter of time before he had to pay the price. The business's future was spent on race horses, exotic places, and sports cars.

Another son inherited his father's furniture business. His dad had been an authoritarian manager, and the son sought to be the same way. It's one thing to be authoritarian and know all the answers, and another to be authoritarian and stupid! He was thoroughly rigid and immoveable. "And that's just the way it is," was his most often heard refrain.

The only problem was that times changed and he stayed the same—he was selling the wrong product to the wrong people.

His authoritarian, rigid approach soon brought him, along with the man in the first example, right down into bankruptcy.

All managers aren't at these two extremes, of course. Most can be found somewhere in between. I've seen a wide variety of styles, leaning either one way or the other, that have been successful and effective.

Success is not found through one particular style. **The critical factor in motivation is not management style—it is the kind of atmosphere the manager creates.** I believe it's virtually impossible for either extreme—the libertarian or the authoritarian—to create the proper working atmosphere for optimum motivation. But in between the extremes it just doesn't much matter what management style you choose. Only the atmosphere it creates is important.

The keys to creating a motivational atmosphere:

• Help everyone involved in the organization have high expectations of it.

• Provide an example of competence by being a competent leader.

• Make people feel that they're important, that they have an impact on the organization, that they make a difference.

• Make sure that all feel a responsibility for company development.

• Make sure the way is open for each individual to grow, both now and in the future.

"Aw, what the hell."

"You're gonna catch hell!"

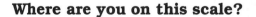

Complete
Libertarian

Complete
Authoritarian

Where are you on this scale?

Setting Goals

One of the very best things a motivator can ever do for his people is to help them set goals. Goals are wondrous and magical: they help a person go from where he is to where he wants to be. Without goals, each person is constantly in need of motivational help from others. **But when a person has goals, he can usually motivate himself.** He is able to move ahead on his own and really do the things that need to be done.

Some steps to setting goals effectively:

• Analyze who and where you are right now.

• Figure out where you want to be. Make the goal specific, and put it in writing.

• Avoid "ungoals"—goals you borrow from someone else, goals that are utterly unrealistic, goals that state what you don't really want, goals that conflict with each other, goals that you aren't willing to work for in order to achieve.

• Rank your goals in the order in which you want to concentrate on them.

• Rewrite your goals as affirmations, positive statements about yourself in terms of where you want to be. Affirmations are written in first-person and in the present tense: "I find three new clients every day."

• Repeat each affirmation every day, and as you do, visually imagine yourself accomplishing it. The mind can't tell the difference between a real experience and a vivid visualization. By visualizing, you'll be able to help your mind know that the goal is realistic.

• After you've visualized the affirmations each day, go out and act as if they were all true. Act as if you have already reached the goal.

• Periodically review where you are and where you're heading. Give yourself feedback to make sure you are on the right course.

Pledge of Allegiance

Our society has been fractured into a million parts. In the past you may have found one or two social organizations per town. Now the figure climbs into the dozens, hundreds, even thousands. People's loyalties are divided between many organizations.

Stratification

Few people offer allegiance to a company as a whole. Instead they give it to the smaller organizations within that company. (See chart)

Such separation of loyalty is probably impossible (and perhaps detrimental!) to completely overcome.

But there are ways to win your employees' loyalty:

• Be aware of each independent group within the company.

• Offer company support to the group. Perhaps you can offer company resources,

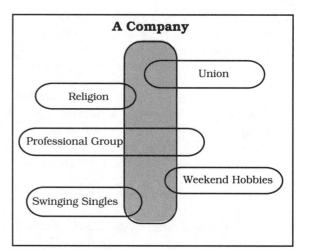

A company usually shares its employees loyalties with diverse groups.

such as facilities for their meetings and gatherings, or pledge funds, products or services during fund-raising activities.

• Sponsor sub-organizations within the company such as teams and tournaments.

Only when people are committed to the company will they be able to give you what you need.

The Weak Link

Any group is only as strong as its weakest link.

And every group has a weak link. Usually it's the misfit, the guy who never gets the hang of things. He's the person who doesn't quite fit in with the others, who doesn't measure up to the expectations of the company. And he never will.

Doesn't Work or Play Well with Others

This weak link is often the fellow of whom it is said: "Doesn't work or play well with others."

To make things worse, the guy is often indifferent to the problem he creates for everyone else in the group.

There is only one solution for the weak link: remove it. Only by removing the weak link will the chain be strengthened. Sometimes you can fix something only by totally replacing it.

Certainly it's never an easy job to tell a worker he has to leave. It's much easier to

There is always one person who will never achieve success, no matter what motivation technique you try.

put the task off, hoping maybe things will improve. But they usually don't—and in the meantime, the entire organization will suffer.

Slowing Down for the Slowest

During World War II, Allied ship convoys had to slow down to the pace of the slowest ship. It seemed like a good idea: if they rushed ahead, the slowest ship would be extremely vulnerable, sitting out there on the water all by itself. There was only one problem. By slowing down, the entire convoy became vulnerable. It became much easier for enemy subs to attack them. The convoy became as weak as its weakest ship.

A manager I know does all he can to avoid confrontation. When he has a weak link, he can see that his production goes down—but still he puts off removing the link. Finally he found some creative ways:

- he gave his secretary (a weak link) a raise—then had his accountant fire her;

- he moved the business to another section of town, leaving a weak link behind;

- he turned his business in another direction, eliminating the job of a weak link.

Even worse is another manager I know: he never removes the weak link. Then he wonders why his other employees don't work up to speed. He never realizes that the "favor" he is doing for the weak worker is a great handicap to all his other workers.

Replaced with Strength

I'm not against any one worker. I'm not saying the misfit should be taken out and shot. He might be a great strength elsewhere. He might be a great neurosurgeon who somehow is stuck in an advertising job. It doesn't matter. Let him serve as a good example of what a bad example is and get him out of there. Bring in a stronger link to replace him. The result will be increased motivation in everyone else.

Who Motivates the Motivator?

The manager's job is to motivate other people. Who motivates the motivator? Few have that assignment, and as they move higher up the ladder, fewer people are in the position to give them motivation.

Two things happen at that point. Either the Peter Principle prevails and the manager flounders in over his head, or he gets himself motivated to the point of success. The first response, of course, spells failure. But if a person can become self-motivated in the truest sense of the word, he will ultimately be able to do anything he sets his mind to. And at that point he can most effectively motivate others.

How does the motivator become self-motivated? It takes effort, but the methods are easy to find.

The same methods that are used to motivate others can be used to motivate yourself. There's only one major difference: apply the motivating factors internally rather than externally.

Any person seeking to motivate himself can, by applying the ideas in this book to his own situation, become completely self-motivated, dependent on no one. And at that point he will be able to motivate others as never before!

Who motivates the motivator? The motivator himself! Any other approach will prove to be unworkable.

Knowledge	+	Goals	+	Strategy Skills	= Desired Results
Knows how to use technical people, outside resources.		*Sets regularly, clear and strong, follows goals untiringly.*		*Solves problems well, plans for both short and long term.*	*The main reson for doing what you are doing—results!*

Feedback

Feedback is a term borrowed from cybernetics and computer design. It is a fundamental fact of existence and a basic concept in science. It is also an essential element in successful motivation. Interestingly, feedback has been recognized as a critical concept only during the last 50 years—and critical it is!

Critical Element of a Directing System

Every goal-oriented system has a feedback mechanism. The mechanism registers the actual state of the system, then compares it to the desired state. Only after the comparison has been made can the mechanism make an adjustment and correct the gap between where the system is and where it should be.

A good example of a feedback mechanism is found in a missile. Feedback tells the missile when it's off course, enabling the missile to make the adjustment that will get it back on target.

Feedback mechanisms tell living cells when to produce protein and when to stop. The feedback part of the system is essential to a healthy cell.

In management, a feedback mechanism (usually you) tells employees how well they are doing toward reaching objectives. Without the mechanism, they're unable to evaluate problems and make adjustments.

The same kind of mechanism works in people situations as well. People under any kind of leader need feedback in order to function well—whether they're adults in some kind of group, students in the classroom, or children in the home.

Here's the key to using feedback in motivation: People need just the right amount of feedback to know how they are doing.

How Do You Determine the Right Amount?

Lack of feedback will cause the system to collapse and die. Without feedback, the worm won't know when it should eat the tomato plant, and it will die of starvation.

Without feedback, employees may stop producing altogether. I know of one company where the boss went on an extended vacation, leaving no provisions for a feedback system while he was gone. When he got back, the employees were gone, and the doors were locked. The employees were unable to perform without feedback.

Scientists in Iran once did a study on children in orphanages. Nurses in the orphanages didn't have time to spend individually with each child—thus the children weren't getting any feedback. Some of them totally withdrew from contact with others, and all developed severe emotional problems.

Then the researchers took some of those children out of the orphanage and placed them in foster homes. In most homes the children received individualized care and attention—and with that kind of feedback they began to grow emotionally and function normally again.

Too much feedback (overgoverning) causes oscillation, then breakdown. For example, when the tolerances of a thermostat are set very tight (overgovernment) the furnaces will continually click on and off until the system breaks down.

When a person becomes too conscious of each element in his speech he begins to stutter. He is suffering from too much feedback.

An employee becomes nervous and starts to make mistakes when his boss stands over him with an eagle eye, watching his every move.

The student whose teacher is always hanging over him is unable to develop on his own. He is so afraid of making a mistake in front of the teacher that he may not progress at all.

With too little feedback, the system misdirects. When a missile receives inadequate feedback, it falls and hits the ground before it even realizes it's off course.

If an employee has too little feedback, he can use up all his resources going in the wrong direction—without having any idea he's making a mistake. Jane's boss asked for a report, but didn't say when it was due. He gave no feedback. In two weeks the boss asked for the report; because of a lack of feedback Jane didn't even know it was due until it was too late.

The same thing happens in groups in general. If the leader gives an assignment, but then fails to give follow-up and provide adequate feedback, the person assigned won't know if his course is correct. He may give it his best shot, but without the feedback, he'll be in the dark about how he's doing. And, in the end, he'll probably find he didn't do exactly what was needed.

Giving only negative or only positive feedback will cause the system to misdirect. The body uses up oxygen at an incredible rate while jogging. If the brain were to tell the respiratory system to keep going at that rate after the body had stopped jogging, a person would soon hyperventilate and pass out.

An isolated Japanese soldier gave himself only positive feedback and continued jungle-fighting for 15 years after World War II was over. Because he hadn't also received negative feedback during that time, it took friendly forces several days to convince him that peace had long since been declared.

The worker who gets only negative feedback will think he can do nothing right. His energies will be directed toward not making mistakes, rather than toward problem solving and production.

The student who gets only positive feedback will think he can do nothing wrong. His work will become sloppy and unacceptable.

Effective Feedback—Just the Right Amount

To give feedback effectively, a motivator needs to keep a good eye on his organization's objectives. With those in mind, he can then help his people see how their individual jobs relate to them. They need to see on a regular basis how they're doing in relation to how they should be doing. Only then will they have the necessary information on how they stand.

Patience Level

$\mathbf{T}$ry this experiment on your small children:"Would you like a cookie right now or a whole package of cookies tomorrow?" Invariably they'll choose the cookie right now! Tomorrow doesn't have a lot of meaning to kids, so they have an incredibly low patience level. If you want to motivate a child give him something right now, because effective motivation is directly linked to patience level.

The patience level of an individual will determine how you should motivate him. The interval and intensity of feedback, rewards, or final benefits should vary according to the person's patience level.

A scientist has spent twenty years on the same research project. He has made few advances and no real breakthroughs. Yet he continues on, motivated. How can he do it? Simply because his patience level is extremely high.

A student completes her final exam, then stalks the halls for hours waiting for the department to post grades and class standings. What is her rush? She has a low patience level.

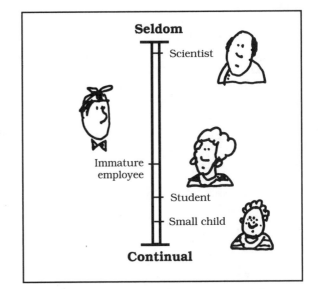

The kind of motivation that will work for each of us depends on our individual patience level.

Misread Level

It's crucial to read the level right when you're motivating others. Top management of one company misread the level of a new middle manager—and it was a critical mistake. When the man was hired, management said they would reward him according to his work: the more the profits, the more he would make and the sooner he'd receive the reward.

The result: the new manager went after short-term benefits without caring for the long-term. The company needed new equipment badly—but that would have hurt his profits. So he chose to forgo the new equipment in favor of his bonus. It was like giving a cookie to a kid. If he had waited, the manager would have gotten much more money in the long run. But he didn't want the box of cookies tomorrow. He wanted the single cookie today, and inadvertently sabotaged tomorrow's productivity.

Determining Each Person's Level

How can you tell what a person's patience level is? The best way is to look at the factors that help form it:

• **Maturity and experience.** Generally, the longer someone has been at something, the higher his patience level.

• **Inner motivation.** Someone who is highly motivated from within usually also has a high patience level.

• **Vision into the future.** The person who sees only tomorrow will be impatient. But the one who has a vision of what things will be like in ten years will have a better perspective—and more patience.

• **Past successes or failures.** Anyone who has experienced a good balance of success and failure will have a higher patience level. Someone who has had too much of one or the other will be impatient when things don't go his way.

It is quite useless to try to change a person's patience level. Only time and experience can do that. But it's essential that a manager understand at what level each of his people operates. If the manager misinterprets, he may well use the wrong kind of motivation with his workers.

A Piece of the Pie

The poor cook! He was always fixing delicious foods, but was never allowed to give any of them a taste! **What baker doesn't work harder when he can have a piece of the pie?**

Company profit-sharing: A method whereby company managers give each worker a piece of the pie. An excellent motivational technique.

"The day is fast coming when the fixed hourly wage will be only a relic of the past in both business and industry," says Jim Goodwin, an executive with Lincoln Electric, one of the pioneers in the field of profit sharing. "The only employees who'll keep on working for a fixed hourly wage will be those employed in nonproductive, non-selling, service type jobs.

"Wage incentive and profit sharing plans have taught us a valuable lesson here at Lincoln Electric. Once you set a realistic quota based on a certain past standard of performance, your men will use every trick they can think of to beat the system so they can have a bigger take-home pay.

Make your workers give all of the pie to everyone else and pretty soon they're not going to want to make such good pie anymore.

"And it's not only money that's at stake. You've challenged his ingenuity and his initiative when you set a standard. In effect, you're saying, 'This is the limit, the ceiling; you can't beat it.' But you just watch him, he will."

From *Guide to Managing People* by James K. Van Fleet.

Key points to pie (profit) sharing:

• Construct a profit-sharing system that fits well in your company. Consider product, style, profit base, and so forth.

• Link performance to rewards—the better the performance, the greater the reward.

• Create a formula that all workers in the company will be able to understand.

• Keep the system fair. Everyone must feel it is totally equitable for all involved!

• Use the system only for rewards, not punishments. Punishment only makes for a mean organization—and who wants to be connected with one of those?

• Keep the lid off. Don't put a ceiling on how much your workers can make. (Too often companies will make a big mistake here. I know a salesperson who was doing very well. She was making as much as the boss—all from commissions. One day the boss called her in: "Jensen, you're doing too well. Now, we can't have you making more than me, so we're going to have to arrange some other approach." So much for motivation!)

One More Point

With profit-sharing, you'll often end up with a lot bigger pie for all involved. But remember: don't have a ceiling on how much the workers can make. Don't worry—whether it's with commissions or profit-sharing, the worker doesn't get more until the company gets more. Don't have a ceiling and everyone's pie will grow!

Human Needs

The more you understand about needs that motivate people, the more effective a motivator you can become.

The core of motivation is meeting needs. If a person's needs are all being met, he's totally satisfied with his situation and isn't open to any kind of change. The satisfied person is generally self-motivated—but if he isn't self-motivated, he'll be pretty hard to motivate.

But who in the world is totally satisfied? No one I've ever met, and probably no one you've ever met either. As long as a person has unmet needs, he can be motivated by having those needs met.

Need Categories

Human needs fit into several categories:

Physiological Needs	**Safety Needs**
Belonging Needs	**Control Needs**
Individual Needs	**Change Needs**
Freedom Needs	**Potential Needs**

Consider your employees, your sales prospects, your students, your children: what needs do they have that you can help them fulfill? As you fill their needs, they'll become motivated to do what you want them to do.

Physiological Needs

Physical, bodily needs are basic to a person's well-being. He needs to keep alive. He needs air, water, sleep, shelter, waste elimination, physical activity.

A person can go without food for sixty days. Life can be sustained without water for seven days. But man can live without oxygen for only three minutes.

If one of these physiological needs is unmet, the person will devote all of his energies to getting it met. In 1943 the U.S. Army conducted a study to see just how vital physiological needs really are. The volunteers were gradually starved until they weighed only two-thirds of their original weight. They were given plenty of food by bulk, but it contained little nutritional value.

As the men progressed through the experiment, their actions changed dramatically. Food became the center of every conversation. They spent a good deal of time talking about great meals they had enjoyed in the past. They described over and over the taste of their favorite foods, in great detail.

When wives came to visit, the men were more interested in talking about food than they were in sex. Pin-ups in the men's lockers were removed, and pictures of sumptuous meals took their place.

When just one of these physiological needs is off-balance, it begins to dominate the thinking and actions of the person. A manager has a hard time motivating the worker who's hungry. But when that hunger is satisfied, as it eventually was in the experiment, the worker is able to turn to other things.

Safety Needs

Even the most macho guy has an aversion to personal harm. Threats get the adrenaline flowing. When our security is threatened, we take decisive and determined steps to set things right again.

The need for security can be seen in a high-crime area. As crime goes up, the amount of production of the community as a whole goes down. Why? Because the people become more concerned about their safety than they are about working effectively.

If one of those employees were to move to a safer area, his production would probably climb.

If an employee who fears heights gets a job working on a scaffolding, watch out! His accomplishment will decrease as time and effort spent on protecting himself increases.

Belonging Needs

Everyone needs to feel loved and accepted by others. We all want to feel part of the group. Grouping is a social instinct.

A company can take advantage of this need and put it to good use. In Japan they're doing exactly that, and the results are quite impressive. Since people need to belong to a group, many foreign firms make the company the group. They help their employees identify with the company and feel an important part of it. The more they feel like they belong with the company the less they feel a need to belong to outside groups.

Dr. Harry Stock, a well-known psychiatrist, identified the intensity of this need: "Loneliness is perhaps the most unbearable of all human emotions."

Control Needs

Control enables us to make sense of our existence. It enables us to make order of things. People seek an understanding of God and religion for this reason. They seek knowledge and competence. The development of habits stems from the desire for order.

When a person sees a picture frame hanging crookedly, almost invariably he'll straighten it. The need for order runs deep and is hard to resist.

Control can also be seen in people's search for their niche in life. The niche represents order; it helps the person develop competence in a particular area; it helps him gain control of that portion of his life.

Individual Needs

We all have a need to be recognized as unique, as individual. I once heard of a young girl who had just moved to a new high school and was having a hard time finding new friends. No one knew who she was. Then one day she ate a worm on a dare. That established her as unique! After that, everyone spoke to her. It was easy to make friends then.

Self-esteem is a vital need in our lives. We want to feel that we are important to others, that we are valuable, that we won't be ignored.

I know of a man who spent most of his life amassing a huge fortune. The millions were added to millions—but still he wasn't satisfied. So then he became a great philanthropist, giving away tremendous sums to worthy causes. Always with one stipulation: that his name be connected to the gift. He wanted to be known as a generous and loving person. His search was to receive recognition as a unique and important person.

Change Needs

Without change we would stagnate and decay. Those who spend their lives trying to create a completely safe and stable environment actually end up building for themselves a prison. We all need new experiences constantly; we need movement emotionally, socially, and intellectually.

A former neighbor's daughter grew up in a stagnant environment—her parents constantly tried to shield her from new experiences. Everything was provided for the girl; she didn't have to learn to do anything. Her parents thought they were doing their child a favor, protecting her from sorrow and pain. But in reality their sterile environment was only denying her a basic need.

After the girl finally left home to go away to college, she had a nervous breakdown. She was unable to cope with the sudden change all at once. To this day she has difficulty providing for even her most basic needs.

McGill University conducted a series of experiments to learn how important new experiences are. Each person was put in a small room, where he stayed throughout the day, except when he had to go to the bath-room. Experimenters controlled the environment so that there was as little sensual stimulation as possible for several days at a time—monotonous sights, sounds, tastes.

The experimenters soon discovered that new experiences are a vital need. When the volunteers were deprived of new stimuli, they began to talk and sing to themselves.

As the deprivation continued, they began hallucinating. When the brain wasn't receiving outside stimuli, it made up its own.

This need can express itself on lower levels as well. The worker who has a monotonous job will spend his time daydreaming instead of paying attention to his work. But when he gets stimulation at work, his involvement—and production—will climb.

Freedom Needs

A basic human need is to feel that one is in control of one's own destiny. We need to feel that we have flexibility of action, multiplicity of choice.

Even small children need control. They love to make choices about their own lives. At the earliest moment they will try to feed themselves (even if they make a total mess of it), dress themselves, choose when they should go to bed.

Adults, of course, are no different. Every person on earth wants to feel like he's free, like he has the power to make his own choices.

If muscles aren't used, they will atrophy and weaken. Likewise, if the will is not exercised, the soul will atrophy and weaken. The personality will become unbalanced and unmet needs for freedom and control will dominate until the situation is rectified.

Potential Needs

No matter to what heights we rise, there's always another step we can take. Progress is a journey, not a destination. We all have an inner potential, and the need to reach for it is basic: we need to progress and develop.

Abraham Maslow called this need self-actualization. Each self needs to feel that it is becoming what it should become. The key is becoming. Simply maintaining an existence is not enough.

The *ficus benjamina*, or Indian fig tree, grows to impressive heights in India. When imported to the United States, it is planted in small pots and kept in an enclosed, indoor environment. As a result the ficus benjamina in the U. S. is only a small potted tree.

If people are put into pots that are too small for their potential, their growth will forever be stunted. Their need for development will be stifled, and they may never become what their potential may have allowed.

An old company man watched as a teenage boy was hired to help out in the company. "Look at that kid, " the old man sneered. "He mumbles all the time and he doesn't look too bright. He'll never amount to much."

But the company allowed its workers to fill the need for developing potential—and now this boy (no longer a boy) leads the company. What happened? Was the old man wrong in his assessment? Probably not. If the boy had remained the way he was when he started with the company, he may never have done much with his life.

But he didn't remain the same. He let himself develop and reach toward his potential.

Any other person in any other company can do the same, when this need is allowed for.

Motivation Is Need Satisfaction

In considering how to motivate your employees through meeting their needs, remember this: when you hire someone, you're not just hiring a hand—the rest of the man has to come with it. The same thing applies to motivation in all situations.

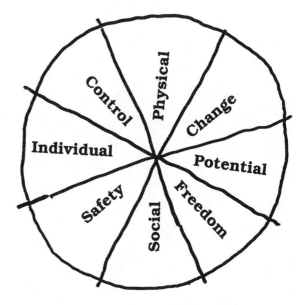

My Size Fits All

Once there was an old tailor who worked deep in the garment district of Manhattan. When customers would come into his shop he would very carefully measure them, marking each measurement on a complex form. Then he would pull a suit off the rack and hand it to them. "Here's your suit," he would say. "Just your size." Of course, customers were always taken aback.

Some would hold the suit up to themselves and see that it was too large or too small. They would notice there was only one color choice. And then, since New Yorkers aren't exactly shy, they'd confront the tailor.

"This isn't my size. I saw you just take it off the rack. Every suit up there is the same, including the one you're wearing. It won't fit me. What are you trying to pull?"

Then the tailor would just smile a little smile and shake his head. "You misunderstand," he would always say. "This is the perfect size for everyone. There is no need for any other suit, because this suit is the ultimate size and color—and it will fit anyone."

Trying to fit everyone into the same mold yields people who don't fit in at all.

What would you think of a tailor who measured his customers and then gave them all only one choice of suit—his?

Rigid Criteria Imposed on All

Unfortunately, motivators often use rigid criteria when evaluating their people. Such criteria attract the few who can fit them— and repel all the others. Except for the favored few, rigid criteria are murder on motivation.

113

"The only person who behaves sensibly is my tailor," said George Bernard Shaw. "He makes new measurements every time he sees me. All the rest go on with their old measurements."

Men to Match My Standards

The president of an accounting firm had very rigid criteria that all his employees had to meet. He was highly touted for successfully finding people to match his standards—for a while.

But then things began to slip. The economic climate changed drastically and the business began to do poorly. The president's restrictive approach had bred out any possibility of new blood. He had been successful only at hiring clones: exact copies of what had gone before. Everyone in the company had the same point of view, the same strengths, the same weaknesses.

Eventually the firm failed. The president hadn't been sensible like Shaw's tailor. Instead he had behaved like the other tailor: "My size fits all."

But of course one size can't fit all. Trying to fit all workers into a set mold won't work—and it won't get the job done either.

Those who want their children or employees to be motivated will let them develop their own personalities and approaches, rather than forcing them into a standard size or style.

"The manager does not primarily seek to solve a problem once and for all or to achieve a single objective. Rather he endeavors to compensate and improvise, constantly to readjust his behavior, marginally, in response to the everchanging environment about him. While seeking stability, holding deviations to a minimum, he can approximate the ideal only by constant change.

"Only managers who can deal with uncertainty, with ambiguity, and with battles that are never won but only fought well can hope to succeed."

Leonard R. Sayles

The most complicated thing in the universe is a human being—and a given person is made even more complicated by each individual uniqueness. Trying to force-fit that uniqueness into a standard mold is one of life's most futile endeavors. It is useless to even try. Making oranges into apples and bananas into grapes is a time-wasting and frustrating experience for all involved. But providing for more natural individual growth can be one of life's most rewarding experiences.

Slices, Dices, and Purées

Order NOW! *This truly incredible AM-FM stereo with tape deck and record turntable, complete with adjustable recording levels, a video-disk player, and alarm clock! Also doubles as a trash compactor!"*

We've all seen TV ads like this. The trouble is that when you over-complicate something or try to make it do everything, it won't do anything well.

More Is Less

We seem to have a strange belief in our culture. We believe that the more things a person or gadget can do, the better it's able to do any one of them. Actually, though, the reverse is what's really true. Multiple demands on a given machine or program or company require that compromises inevitably be made. Sure, it's possible to make a bathtub that doubles as a lawnmower, but the resulting contraption will neither cut nor clean well.

- Congress is trying to pass a bill. Every Congressman and his dog says he'll vote for the bill—if you'll just agree to a small

When you try to make people, things, or ideas do everything, you end up with them doing nothing well.

rider he wants to attach to it. So the bill passes. But with so many little clauses, no one knows what it does. No one knows how to interpret it. The bill tried to be all things to all people—and lost its purpose. It ended up being nothing to anyone.

- A company produces an electric razor, and does a darn good job of it. Then they add a pre-shave lotion to their product line, and things start to get complicated. Next comes an after-shave, then a men's line of shaving robes. Pretty soon the company doesn't even do a good job with the razor.

• The salesman does well at his job. In fact, month after month he's the top guy. "He does so well," management says, "let's make him a supervisor, in addition to his selling duties. We'll pay him extra for it." One problem: things are getting complicated.

The Swiss Army Knife

This is called the Swiss Army Knife Approach to Management. It's a great killer of motivation and progress. It takes the good things in a company and slaps them dead by trying to do too many things. It may get more things done, but quality and proficiency invariably suffer.

The simpler the approach, the more effective it will be. The more effective an approach, the more positive the results.

When working with and motivating people, remember that simple is better. This applies to goals, instruction, assignments—virtually everything.

Maslow's Hierarchy of Needs

Abraham Maslow was the father of the human potential movement. He spent years researching the healthy personality (most study only the abnormal), and he learned that all of us have the same basic needs. These needs always come in the same order, for everyone on earth. The second-level need cannot really be considered until the first-level need is met. The third-level need will become an important priority when the first and second levels are taken care of. And so on.

Here is Maslow's hierarchy of needs, widely accepted by psychologists, motivational experts, and managers around the world:

Self-actualization Needs Being able to reach one's potential, to grow, to progress. This need can never be sought until all the other needs are met.

Esteem Needs Feeling important, useful, competent, needed by others.

Acceptance Needs Having love, friends, intimacy, contact with others.

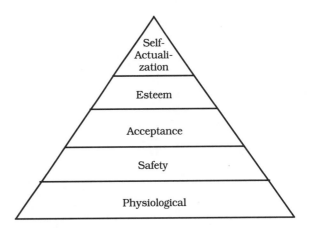

Safety Needs Security, stability, freedom from fear.

Physiological Needs Food, drink, shelter, sex, and so on. If a person doesn't ever have these needs met, he'll never move onto the next level of need.

Organizational Failures

Most organizations don't even try to meet the higher needs (acceptance, esteem, self-actualization). Instead they simply give the worker money to use on his physiological needs and offer him job security in an effort to meet the safety need. By ignoring other needs, the organization loses a good opportunity to motivate its workers; they go elsewhere to have their needs met.

Some managers don't even meet lower-level needs well. If a manager is hung up on the use and abuse of power, his people will feel insecure and will never get past the safety need level.

In dealing with needs, there's one complicating factor: in a given organization, there are usually many different people at several different levels of need.

Needs are at the center of motivating others. The simple fact is that people are motivated only through the satisfaction of their needs. As a manager learns to meet the needs of his workers, he learns how to motivate in ways that will get the job done.

Balanced Motivation

How is a forklift operator like a green cucumber?

All living things, including man, are governed by the biological concept called homeostasis.

The forklift operator adjusts his lift according to the load. He also eats according to his energy consumption, to keep himself alive.

The green cucumber consumes water to maintain balance with its leaf evaporation. It adjusts the way its leaves face the sun according to the amount of photosynthesis that's needed.

Homeostasis—Equilibrium, Balance, Steady State

Homeostasis is the dynamic maintenance of equilibrium or balance in living organisms. The objective of all organisms is to maintain a constant and steady state of being. When the system perceives a change in equilibrium, it makes adjustments to restore the balance.

People are highly motivated by the need to have balance in their lives. The manager can give them just the right things to keep them steady on the high wire.

The principle of homeostasis is as applicable to humans as it is to worms or elm trees. A manager can motivate his people by helping them to balance the fulfillment of all their needs.

119

Governing All Living Things

• A one-celled protozoan has a preferred or optimal temperature at which it thrives. The cell always monitors its own temperature, and when that changes it quickly takes steps to regain the optimum.

• A man gets hungry. That hunger begins to dominate him. Finally he finds a place to eat. He gets the food he needs—and now that he's satisfied he drives away and turns to other concerns.

• A business experiences a drop in cash flow and begins to feel the pinch. Managers apply pressure to marketing to increase sales. Sales go up and cash flow increases. Managers then release the pressure and things return to a state much as before the crisis.

• A ditch-digger gets hot. To restore balance, the body gives off water in the form of sweat, which evaporates from the skin.

The surface temperature drops. Once the body is sufficiently cooled, the sweating stops.

Homeostasis and Homo Sapiens

Every organism on earth is complex, and man is the most complex of all. He seeks homeostasis not only physically, but also emotionally. That's one reason he's sometimes so tough to motivate; while his boss is trying to get him to do one thing, he's off trying to restore his balance with something else.

Homeostasis is such a basic principle that there's no way any person can overrule it. So we should use it to motivate people. If someone needs to improve, whether it be performance or production, match improvement to the fulfillment of one of his needs. Then, as an individual's needs are met and his balance maintained, his well-being and that of his co-workers will collectively improve performance of the entire group.

The Picture Puzzle of Skills

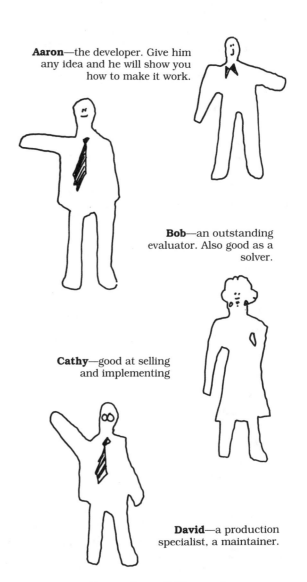

Aaron—the developer. Give him any idea and he will show you how to make it work.

Bob—an outstanding evaluator. Also good as a solver.

Cathy—good at selling and implementing

David—a production specialist, a maintainer.

Numerous skills are needed to effectively run a business. But no one has them all. People have different skills in differing amounts. Managers must find people who have the skills they need, then fit them together.

A Winning Combination

Here are the basic skills the manager will look for. Note that the labels I use don't follow the usual job descriptions:

Creator An originator, an inventor of things or ideas. This person comes up with ideas but doesn't follow through.

Developer The person who takes ideas and develops them into something real and usable.

Implementer The person who puts the developed idea into its real-world context, who gets it going in the process.

Seller The person who sells the idea to others.

Each person has unique skills, and no one has every skill a company needs. The answer is to find the combination of skills that is needed in your company.

121

Maintainer The person who keeps the management or production or distribution of the idea going.

Evaluator The person who judges how well the results match the purpose.

Solver The person who locates and defines problems and proposes solutions.

Nobody Has It All

All of these skills are necessary. One person may be two parts developer and one part seller, with absolutely no skills as a maintainer. Another person may be a creator supreme—but he's no good for anything else.

Each of these people has different skills in different amounts. The key is to fit them together like a puzzle, so that as an overall team they accomplish what needs to be done.

Team—A Combination of Needed Skills

The idea of team is essential. The manager doesn't want several different people working independently in their own little corners. He wants a group working together on an overall problem—a team.

The motivational problem can be fit into three steps:

1. Evaluate who does what and how well they do it. This involves all measurement of realities and possibilities.

2. Give each person the job that best fits his or her skills and talents. Channel skills toward the greatest productivity and job satisfaction.

3. Put each person in the right combination with others. Get the maximum use of the combined skills.

By following these three steps, a manager can fit the pieces of his puzzle together to get the most out of his people. He doesn't require that each person be all things to all people—he lets each of his employees do what he does best and has others fill in the gaps.

The three-step approach will work. But the manager needs to have the proper skills to be able to apply it. **Do you have the needed skills?**

Fit your people together like a puzzle and you will have a united team that can give everything you want.

Towards A Higher Level of Achievement

The sales department hadn't been performing as desired. So in order to get those sales figures up, the department was divided into separate competing areas. Each one was pitted against the other for trips, bonuses, resources, and the attention of top management.

Sales figures started off with a bang—things never looked better. But as time went on, sales took a consistently downward turn.

Rivalries escalated. Backbighting became common and sabotage was increasing. On the surface, smiles and words sounded just right, but underneath it all resentment was building, and teamwork and trust were disappearing.

A new manager was brought in, and the first thing he did was dissolve the competing groups. Rivals were assigned to work together on a project, the reward system was changed to reflect cooperation over competition, and workspaces were rearranged to prevent possible "regrouping". After three long months, a cooperative foundation had been established. Profitability rose, cooperative growth in the entire department in-

Stiff competition poorly managed can bring progress to a halt.

creased, even stress-related absences and insurance claims decreased. This time the sales improvements were lasting.

The long-term cost of this unfortunate scenario was enormous, but caught in time. Other organizations are not so lucky. When fierce competition is allowed to run free, it can destroy everything in its path like a wild brush fire.

Extreme competition can result in disintegration and failure.

To the American mind, competion fits right in with individual freedom and apple pie. Success in any venture is winning, and winning means one wins and others lose. Doing something well means that you must beat out someone. As you move upward someone else falls back. Right?

Contrast this with the Japanese approach. They succeed by cooperation, with an emphasis on maintaining harmony and consensus. The time it takes to foster these values drives Americans mad. But the results have shown it pays off.

For example, it may take a U.S. car company five years or more to design and produce a new car. Turf battles within the company are common, as each area of specialty seeks its own best interest. In contrast, Japanese car companies have been designing and producing new models in as little as eighteen months. And they do it without the stress of internal competition. This ability to respond faster continues to be a major competitive advantage for the Japanese in the world market.

As a kid, I happened upon two cock pheasants fighting one day. The struggle was fierce, feathers were flying everywhere. The self-absorbed competitors didn't even notice me. Nor did they notice the two hawks circling overhead, then diving. When the fight was over, the hawks were the only winners.

These birds were so intent on their own fight that they lost sight of the larger environment and any threat that could come from it. They not only lost their turf, they lost their lives.

Success often depends on the wise use of limited resources and an awareness of the larger environment. Internal competition discourages both conservation of resources and awareness of the larger context. Resources and attention are diverted to the fight for one-upmanship, to looking better than the next guy.

Competition is innate in all living things and their relationships, but, like most things, when carried to an extreme it is destructive.

The dangers of competition can be illustrated by a liferaft at sea after a ship has sunk. The boat is loaded with people glad they are alive and hopeful for a quick rescue. After a few very stressful days, a fight breaks out over which direction to head. The arguing escalates into physical violence, and during a skirmish a hole is accidentally punched in the bottom of the boat. Competition has destroyed their very means of survival.

Positive cooperation promotes growth and allows a higher level of achievement.

The kind of competition I am talking about is rarely beneficial. Beating somebody out is very different from refining expertise or improving output. While the former focuses on defeating (or even eliminating) the competition, the latter concentrates on improving yourself, doing your best. In the long run, the latter attitude will strengthen your work force, encourage excellence, and foster success.